Nelson Secondary
Maths Extension

Nelson

Thomas Nelson and Sons Ltd
Nelson House Mayfield Road
Walton-on-Thames Surrey
KT12 5PL UK

Thomas Nelson Australia
102 Dodds Street
South Melbourne
Victoria 3205 Australia

Nelson Canada
1120 Birchmount Road
Scarborough Ontario
MIK 5G4 Canada

First published by Thomas Nelson and Sons Ltd 1997
I(T)P Thomas Nelson is an International Thomson Publishing Company
I(T)P is used under licence

ISBN 0-17-431463-9
NPN 9 8 7 6 5 4 3 2 1

Printed in Croatia

Nelson Secondary Maths Extension is written by:

Jim Noonan (Series Coordinator)
Paula Barker
Terry Bevis
Gay Cain
Brian Martin
Christine Mitchell
Robert Powell
Gwen Wood

The authors are grateful for advice received from schools in Avon, Birmingham, Cornwall, Cumbria, Essex, Gloucestershire, Gwent, Hampshire, Hereford & Worcester, Nottingham, Salford, South Glamorgan, Tyneside and Wiltshire involved in trials of material for this series.

Contents

Preface v

1 Powers and roots 1

Multiplying and dividing by negative numbers • Cubes and cube roots • Powers

2 Further algebra 14

Multiplying algebraic expressions • Factorising • Dividing with algebraic terms • Changing the subject

3 Pythagoras and proof 26

Using Pythagoras' Theorem • Proving Pythagoras' Theorem • Pythagorean triples

4 Comparing data 36

Considering the spread • Cumulative frequency • Quartiles • Box plots

5 Introduction to trigonometry 46

Tangents • Triangles and tangents • Sines, cosines and triangles • Practical uses of trigonometry

6 Solving simultaneous equations 61

Solving simultaneous equations using graphs • Solving by substitution • Solving by elimination

7 What are my chances? 72

Tree diagrams • Independent events • Mutually exclusive events

8 Quadratic curves 84

Drawing curves • Parabolas • Drawing graphs of parabolas • Sketching graphs

Answers to exercises 93

Preface

It is not intended that this book be treated as following straight on from Book 3, but rather as an additional resource for those pupils who are able to cope confidently with the related material in Book 3.

There are eight chapters, some of which take aspects of the Key Stage 3 curriculum further into Level 8. The style differs slightly from the other Key Stage 3 books of Nelson Mathematics in that more examples are included in each chapter.

- Chapter 1 extends the work on powers and roots and looks at the effect of multiplying and dividing negative numbers.
- Chapter 2 looks at factorising and expanding algebraic expressions as well as the manipulation of equations.
- The application of Pythagoras' Theorem in both two and three dimensions is considered in Chapter 3.
- Chapter 4 shows how data can be compared using two new methods: cumulative frequency and box plots.
- Chapter 5 introduces tangents, sines and cosines, and then uses these trigonometric ratios to solve problems involving right-angled triangles.
- A second visit to algebra occurs in Chapter 6, this time looking at ways of solving simultaneous equations.
- Chapter 7, on probability, follows up on the work from Book 3 and introduces the technique of tree diagrams as a means of displaying the probability of a combination of events.
- Chapter 8 introduces the family of curves related to $y = x^2$.

At this level of work, it is expected that pupils have access to either a scientific or graphic calculator. Indeed several of the chapters make specific reference to the use of these types of calculators.

Each chapter of the book is intended to stand alone, and it is quite appropriate for a pupil to use this book for selected chapters only. However, the book should not be used as a self-taught text. The input from the teacher is important.

CHAPTER 1

Powers and roots

In this chapter you will learn:

- → **more about negative numbers**
- → **more about powers and roots.**

You will find it useful to have a scientific calculator for some of the work in this chapter.

Starting points

Before starting this chapter, you will need to know:

- the notation for squares and square roots and how to calculate them
- how to find fractions of quantities
- how to multiply one fraction by another.

Exercise 1

1 Find the value of these *without* using a calculator.

(a) 4^2 (b) 11^2 (c) 20^2

(d) $\sqrt{25}$ (e) $\sqrt{81}$ (f) $\sqrt{225}$

2 Use a calculator to find the value of these.

(a) 24^2 (b) 1.6^2 (c) $\sqrt{289}$

(d) $\sqrt{3.61}$ (e) $\sqrt{32}$ (f) $\sqrt{28}$

3 Use a method of trial and improvement to estimate the value of $\sqrt{45}$ correct to one decimal place.

Use the √ key on your calculator to check your result.

4 There are 950 children in a school. Three-fifths of them are boys.

(a) How many of them are boys?

(b) How many of them are girls?

5 Of the 504 houses on an estate, two-ninths are detached, four-ninths are semi-detached and the rest are bungalows.

Find the number of each type of house.

6 In a box of 168 apples delivered to a shop, half are found to be damaged and half of those remaining are too small to sell.

(a) How many apples can be sold?

(b) What fraction of the apples in the box can be sold?

7 A child receives £2.40 pocket money.

He saves three-quarters of the money and spends three-quarters of that remaining on sweets.

(a) How much does the child save?

(b) How much does the child spend on sweets?

(c) What fraction of the pocket money is spent on sweets?

8 Find the value of these squares, giving your answers as fractions.

(a) $\left(\frac{1}{2}\right)^2$ (b) $\left(\frac{1}{5}\right)^2$ (c) $\left(\frac{3}{4}\right)^2$

(d) $\left(\frac{2}{3}\right)^2$ (e) $\left(\frac{1}{10}\right)^2$ (f) $\left(\frac{1}{100}\right)^2$

9 Find the value of these square roots, giving your answers as fractions.

(a) $\sqrt{\left(\frac{1}{25}\right)}$ (b) $\sqrt{\left(\frac{1}{9}\right)}$ (c) $\sqrt{\left(\frac{1}{36}\right)}$

(d) $\sqrt{\left(\frac{4}{9}\right)}$ (e) $\sqrt{\left(\frac{4}{25}\right)}$ (f) $\sqrt{\left(\frac{49}{64}\right)}$

Multiplying and dividing by negative numbers

Assignment 1 Building a multiplication table

- Make a copy of this table.

×	−4	−3	−2	−1	0	1	2	3	4
4					0	4	8	12	16
3						3	6	9	12
2						2	4	6	8
1								3	4
0									
−1									
−2									
−3									
−4									

- Look for sequences to help you to complete the table.
- Use the information in the completed table to devise a rule for multiplying two negative numbers.

Exercise 2

> Write down the calculation *and* the answer for each question in this exercise.

1 Use the completed table from Assignment 1 to help you to work out the answers to these multiplications.

(a) 3×-1 (b) 2×-4 (c) -3×3
(d) -4×-2 (e) 0×-4 (f) -4×-3
(g) -3×-3 (h) -4×-4 (i) $-(2)^2$

2 From the table you can see that if $2 \times 3 = 6$ then $6 \div 2 = 3$ and $6 \div 3 = 2$. Write down the answers to these divisions and then use your completed table to check your answers.

(a) $12 \div 4$ (b) $16 \div 4$ (c) $3 \div 1$ (d) $0 \div 4$

3 Use your table to work out the answers to these divisions.

(a) $-6 \div -2$ (b) $-12 \div 4$ (c) $16 \div -4$ (d) $-16 \div 2$
(e) $-12 \div -3$ (f) $-8 \div -2$ (g) $0 \div -2$ (h) $-1 \div -1$

4 Use a calculator to check your answers to Questions 1 and 3.

> You will need to use the +/– key to enter negative numbers on your calculator.

Key fact

When you multiply a positive number by a negative number you obtain a negative result.

$(+) \times (-) = (-)$
$(-) \times (+) = (-)$

When you multiply a negative number by a negative number you obtain a positive result.

$(-) \times (-) = (+)$

5 Use any observations you have made about the patterns in the table or your answers to Questions 1 and 3 to predict the answers to these.

(a) -7×3 (b) -8×-4 (c) -6×5 (d) -10×-10
(e) 20×-2 (f) $8 \div -2$ (g) $-8 \div 2$ (h) $-8 \div -2$
(i) $-9 \div 3$ (j) $0 \div -10$ (k) $-27 \div -3$ (l) -6×100

6 Use the key facts about multiplication to answer these questions.

(a) 5×-10 (b) -3×-2 (c) -6×-1 (d) -8×5
(e) 0×-9 (f) -2×5 (g) -1×16 (h) -4×-8

7 Use the key facts about division to answer these questions.

(a) $-5 \div -1$ (b) $-12 \div 1$ (c) $9 \div -3$ (d) $-14 \div -2$
(e) $0 \div -6$ (f) $-8 \div -4$ (g) $-20 \div -4$ (h) $400 \div -4$

8 Use the key facts about division to answer these questions.

(a) $\frac{6}{-2}$ (b) $\frac{-4}{-2}$ (c) $\frac{-27}{3}$ (d) $\frac{0}{-7}$

(e) $\frac{-18}{6}$ (f) $\frac{-70}{-5}$ (g) $\frac{-28}{-4}$ (h) $\frac{-45}{-9}$

9 Use the key facts about multiplication to answer these questions.

(a) -6×-6 (b) -5×-5 (c) -7×-7 (d) -8×-8
(e) $(-3)^2$ (f) $(-10)^2$ (g) $(-40)^2$ (h) $(-15)^2$

10 Write down two values for each of these.

(a) $\sqrt{25}$ (b) $\sqrt{100}$ (c) $\sqrt{1}$

Key fact

Division follows the same rules as multiplication.

$(+) \div (-) = (-)$
$(-) \div (+) = (-)$
$(-) \div (-) = (+)$

11 (a) 2×-9 (b) -5×-6 (c) $4 \div -1$ (d) $-10 \div -2$

(e) $\frac{70}{-2}$ (f) $\frac{-81}{-9}$ (g) $-4 \div \frac{1}{2}$ (h) $-\frac{1}{4} \times -\frac{1}{2}$

(i) $(-12)^2$ (j) $\left(-\frac{1}{2}\right)^2$ (k) $\left(-\frac{1}{4}\right)^2$ (l) $\left(-\frac{3}{4}\right)^2$

12 Is it possible to find a value for $\sqrt{-25}$? Explain your answer.

Cubes and cube roots

The volume of this cube is $3\text{cm} \times 3\text{cm} \times 3\text{cm} = 27\text{cm}^3$.

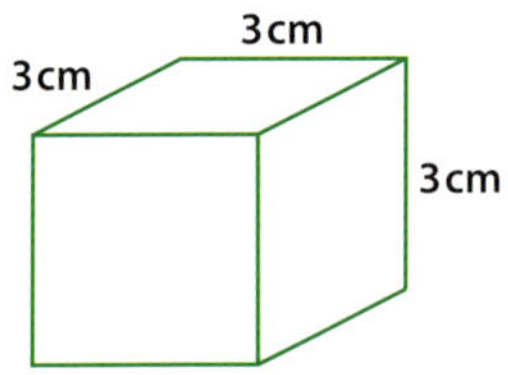

Volume of a cube = length × width × height

You read this as '27 centimetres cubed'.

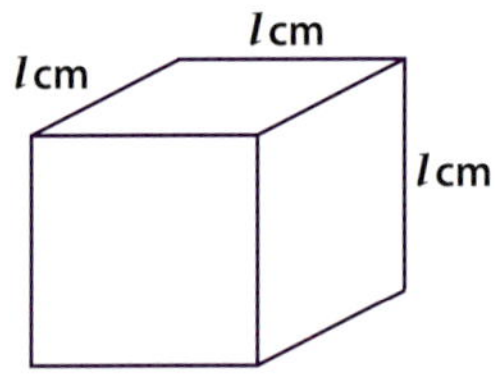

If the length of each side of this cube is l cm, a formula for its volume (V) is

$V = l \times l \times l$

If the volume is 8cm^3, then

$l^3 = 8$

and

$l = 2$

because $2 \times 2 \times 2 = 8$. The answer is the cube root of 8.

$8 = 2 \times 2 \times 2$
$\sqrt[3]{8} = 2$

Exercise 3

1 (a) Complete this table to give the volume of different sized cubes.

Length of side l (cm)	0	1	2	3	4	5	6	7	8
Volume of cube V (cm^3)	0		8						

(b) Use the results in the table to draw the graph of $V = l^3$ on graph paper. Use a scale of 2cm to every 1cm for l and 2cm to every 100cm^3 for V.

(c) Use the graph to estimate V when $l = 4.5$cm.

(d) Use the graph to estimate the value of l when $V = 325\text{cm}^3$.

(e) Copy and complete this sentence.

$\sqrt[3]{325}$ is approximately _____ .

2 Work out the value of these cubes.

(a) 12^3 (b) 15^3 (c) 18^3 (d) 2.5^3

(e) $\left(\frac{1}{2}\right)^3$ (f) $\left(\frac{1}{10}\right)^3$ (g) $\left(\frac{2}{5}\right)^3$ (h) 0^3

3 Work out the value of these cube roots.

(a) $\sqrt[3]{64}$ (b) $\sqrt[3]{125}$ (c) $\sqrt[3]{216}$ (d) $\sqrt[3]{1000}$

(e) $\sqrt[3]{\frac{1}{27}}$ (f) $\sqrt[3]{\frac{1}{8}}$ (g) $\sqrt[3]{\frac{1}{1000}}$ (h) $\sqrt[3]{\frac{27}{125}}$

4 Write down the value of $\sqrt[3]{8}$ and $\sqrt[3]{27}$.

Use the method of trial and improvement to estimate $\sqrt[3]{12}$ correct to 1 decimal place.

5 Work out the value of these.

(a) $-3 \times -3 \times -3$ (b) $-5 \times -5 \times -5$ (c) $-6 \times -6 \times -6$ (d) $-7 \times -7 \times -7$

(e) $(-4)^3$ (f) $(-1)^3$ (g) $(-8)^3$ (h) $(-10)^3$

6 Find the value of these.

(a) $\sqrt[3]{-8}$ (b) $\sqrt[3]{-125}$ (c) $\sqrt[3]{-1}$ (d) $\sqrt[3]{-27}$

Powers

Assignment 2 Building pyramids

A pyramid can be built using square layers of cubical blocks.

- How many cubes will be needed for the bottom layer in a pyramid with eight layers?
- How many layers will a pyramid consisting of 30 cubes have?
- Investigate the number of blocks needed to build pyramids of different sizes.

Assignment 3 Folding

You need a sheet of thin A4 paper for this assignment.

- Fold the paper in half. Open out the paper again. How many sections are there?
- Fold the paper in half as before, then fold it in half again. How many sections do you think there will be this time?
- Copy and complete this table to show how many sections the paper will be divided into when you fold it a given number of times.

Number of folds (x)	0	1	2	3	4	5
Number of sections (s)		2				

- Predict how many sections you would have for six folds of the paper.
- Predict how many folds you would have if the paper was divided into 128 sections.
- Is there a limit to the number of folds possible? Investigate!
- Try to find a formula connecting s and x.

Powers of positive numbers

Powers can be used to write calculations in a shorter way. For example

$4 \times 4 \times 4 = 4^3$

Here are some more examples:

$2^5 = 2 \times 2 \times 2 \times 2 \times 2$

$5 \times 5 \times 5 \times 5 = 5^4$

$\left(\frac{1}{2}\right)^3 = \frac{1}{2} \times \frac{1}{2} \times \frac{1}{2}$

$2 \times 2 \times 5 \times 5 \times 5 = 2^2 \times 5^3$

> Powers can be used to write in shorthand form the value of a number multiplied by itself a given number of times.

Exercise 4

1 Write down each of these in a simpler way, using powers.
(Do not write down the answer to the calculation.)

(a) $2 \times 2 \times 2 \times 2$
(b) $5 \times 5 \times 5$
(c) $8 \times 8 \times 8 \times 8 \times 8 \times 8 \times 8$
(d) $10 \times 10 \times 10 \times 10$
(e) $2.1 \times 2.1 \times 2.1$
(f) $20 \times 20 \times 20 \times 20 \times 20$

2 Write each of these in a simpler way, using powers.

(a) $2 \times 2 \times 2 \times 3 \times 3 \times 3 \times 3$ (b) $4 \times 4 \times 5 \times 5 \times 5$

(c) $6 \times 6 \times 6 \times 7 \times 7 \times 7 \times 7 \times 2 \times 2$ (d) $2 \times 3 \times 5 \times 3 \times 2 \times 5 \times 2$

(e) $7 \times 6 \times 2 \times 6 \times 6 \times 7$ (f) $2 \times 2 \times 4 \times 4 \times 5 \times 6$

3 Find the value of each of these.

(a) 5^2 (b) 2^8 (c) 3^4

(d) 6^4 (e) 10^6 (f) 4^4

(g) $\left(\frac{1}{4}\right)^2$ (h) $\left(\frac{1}{5}\right)^3$ (i) $\left(\frac{2}{3}\right)^4$

4 Find the value of each of these.

(a) $2^2 \times 3^3$ (b) $5^2 \times 4^3$ (c) $2^3 \times 5^3$

(d) $7^2 \times 10^4$ (e) $\left(\frac{1}{2}\right)^2 \times 2^3$ (f) $\left(\frac{1}{3}\right)^4 \times 3^4$

5 What number must be written instead of each x to make each of these statements true?

(a) $2^x = 16$ (b) $3^x = 27$ (c) $5^x = 625$

(d) $\left(\frac{1}{2}\right)^x = \frac{1}{32}$ (e) $\left(\frac{1}{3}\right)^x = \frac{1}{81}$ (f) $(0.1)^x = 0.001$

6 In this diagram, all the shapes are enlargements of shape A.

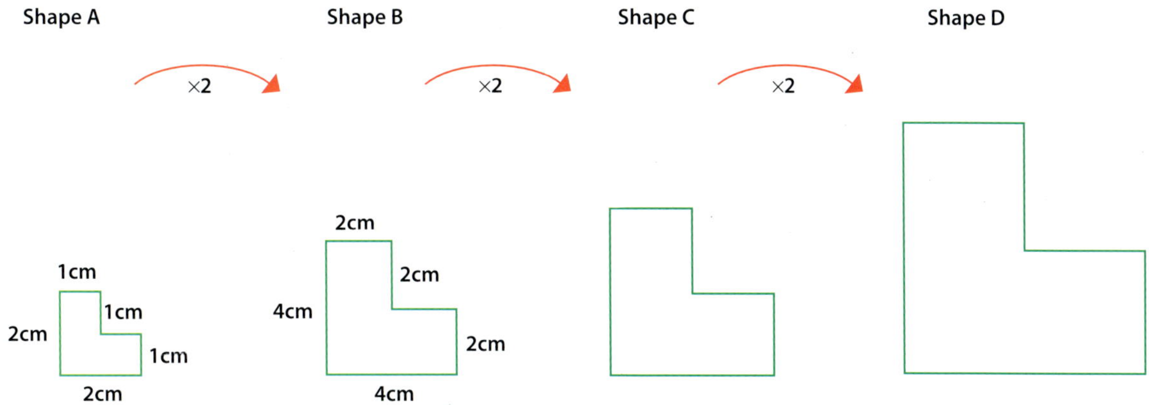

(a) Draw shape D to scale.

(b) What is the scale factor of the enlargement that maps shape A on to shape D?

7 A child has 64 sweets.

She gives half of the sweets to a friend.

She gives half of those she has left to her sister and, of those remaining, she gives half to her dog.

(a) How many sweets does she give away?

(b) What fraction of the sweets does she give to her dog?

Assignment 4 Sequences

- Copy out these sequences and write down the next three numbers in each one.

2, 4, 8, ...

5, 25, 125, ...

10, 100,1000, ...

0.1, 0.01, 0.001, ...

$\frac{1}{2}, \frac{1}{4}, \frac{1}{8}, \ldots$

$\frac{1}{3}, \frac{1}{9}, \frac{1}{27}, \ldots$

- Write down the terms in each sequence again, this time using powers.
- Write down a rule for finding the *n*th term in each sequence.
- For each sequence, describe what happens to each term as *n* gets larger.

Using a scientific calculator when working with powers and roots

There are keys on a scientific calculator which will help you to avoid putting in repeated calculations.

Powers of any numbers can be found using the key labelled in the form x^y.

Many calculators also have x^3 and $\sqrt[3]{}$ keys to help you to work out cubes and cube roots.

Experiment with some simple examples to check that you know how to use your calculator when working with powers and roots. Then, using a scientific calculator, find the quickest method for finding the value of each expression given in Exercise 5.

Write down the question *and* answer for each question.

Exercise 5

1 (a) 9^3 (b) 11^3 (c) 18^3
(d) 2.6^3 (e) 1.2^3 (f) 0.7^3

2 (a) 2^{12} (b) 5^7 (c) 11^4
(d) 0.5^5 (e) 3^9 (f) 6^6

3 (a) $\sqrt[3]{512}$ (b) $\sqrt[3]{9261}$ (c) $\sqrt[3]{4096}$

4 (a) $8^3 \times 4^2$ (b) $5^4 \times 7^2$ (c) $8^3 \times 3^4$
(d) $0.2^3 \times 4^5$ (e) $6^3 \times 10^4$ (f) $4.5^3 \times 2^5$
(g) $\frac{3^5 \times 2^3}{5^2}$ (h) $\frac{5^6 \times 3^5}{2^4}$ (i) $\frac{4^3 \times 5^2}{5^4}$

Simplifying calculations without using a calculator

Calculations involving powers can often be simplified *without* using a calculator. Here are some examples.

$2^3 \times 2^4 = (2 \times 2 \times 2) \times (2 \times 2 \times 2 \times 2) = 2^7$

$3^5 \times 3^3 = (3 \times 3 \times 3 \times 3 \times 3) \times (3 \times 3 \times 3) = 3^8$

$\frac{4^5}{4^2} = \frac{4 \times 4 \times 4 \times 4 \times 4}{4 \times 4} = 4^3$

$(5^3)^2 = 5^3 \times 5^3 = 5^6$

In Exercise 6, simplify (but do not calculate) the values of the expressions.

Exercise 6

1 (a) $2^5 \times 2^2$ (b) $5^3 \times 5^2 \times 5$ (c) $8^3 \times 8^2 \times 8^2$

(d) $10^2 \times 10^4$ (e) $3^5 \times 3^4$ (f) $4^3 \times 4^4$

(g) $7^3 \times 7^2 \times 7^4$ (h) $\left(\frac{1}{2}\right)^2 \times \left(\frac{1}{2}\right)^4 \times \left(\frac{1}{2}\right)^3$ (i) $(0.1)^3 \times (0.1)^5 \times (0.1)^7$

2 (a) $\frac{6^4}{6^2}$ (b) $\frac{5^3}{5^2}$ (c) $\frac{13^8}{13^5}$

(d) $\frac{10^4}{10^2}$ (e) $\frac{3^3}{3^3}$ (f) $\frac{(7^2 \times 7^4)}{7^3}$

(g) $\frac{4^{10}}{4^5 \times 4^5}$ (h) $\frac{3^7}{3^2 \times 3^4}$ (i) $\frac{5^{40}}{5^{10} \times 5^{10}}$

3 (a) $(4^2)^3$ (b) $(5^3)^2$ (c) $(2^3)^3$

(d) $(7^5)^2$ (e) $(10^2)^4$ (f) $(3^4)^3$

(g) $\left(\left(\frac{1}{2}\right)^2\right)^3$ (h) $\left(\left(\frac{1}{3}\right)^3\right)^2$ (i) $((0.1)^2)^4$

4 (a) $2^3 \times 3^4 \times 3^5$ (b) $5^2 \times 5^4 \times 7^2$ (c) $2^5 \times 2^2 \times 4^3 \times 4^4$

5 (a) $\frac{(7^2)^3 \times 7^5}{7^4}$ (b) $\frac{((5^3)^2 \times (5^2)^3)}{5^3}$ (c) $\frac{((4^3)^3 \times (5^2)^2)}{4^4}$

Powers of negative numbers

When a negative number is multiplied by itself several times, shorthand notation can be used as before.

Examples

$-1 \times -1 \times -1 \times -1 = (-1)^4$

$-4 \times -4 \times -4 = (-4)^3$

You must think carefully about the signs when working out the value of these.

$$\begin{aligned}(-1)^4 &= -1 \times -1 \times -1 \times -1 \\ &= \underbrace{(-1 \times -1)}_{+1} \times \underbrace{(-1 \times -1)}_{+1} \\ &= +1 \times +1 \\ &= +1\end{aligned}$$

The value of $(-1)^4$ is 1.

$$\begin{aligned}(-4)^3 &= -4 \times -4 \times -4 \\ &= \underbrace{(-4 \times -4)}_{+16} \times -4 \\ &= +16 \times -4 \\ &= -64\end{aligned}$$

The value of $(-4)^3$ is –64.

Check these results on your calculator.

Exercise 7

1 Write down each of these in a simpler way, using powers.
(Do not write the answer to the calculation.)

(a) $-2 \times -2 \times -2 \times -2 \times -2$ (b) $-7 \times -7 \times -7$
(c) $-10 \times -10 \times -10 \times -10$ (d) $-4 \times -4 \times -4$

2 Without using a calculator, work out the value of each of these.

(a) $(-5)^3$ (b) $(-2)^6$ (c) $(-3)^3$ (d) $(-1)^5$
(e) $(-8)^2$ (f) $(-10)^6$ (g) $(-1)^6$ (h) $(-100)^3$

3 Use a calculator to work out each of these.

(a) $(-5)^5$ (b) $(-3)^6$ (c) $(-12)^4$ (d) $(-7)^3$
(e) $(-1.5)^4$ (f) $(-2.4)^3$ (g) $(0.7)^2$ (h) $(-0.01)^3$

4 Write down each of these in a simpler way.
(Do not work out the answer to each calculation.)

(a) $(-3)^2 \times (-3)^4$ (b) $(-4)^3 \times (-4)^4$ (c) $(-5)^4 \times (-5)^3$ (d) $(-2)^4 \times (-2)^5$
(e) $(-2)^4 \times (-2)^8$ (f) $((-2)^3)^4$ (g) $((-3)^2)^3$ (h) $((-4)^2)^2$
(i) $\frac{(-4)^3}{-4}$ (j) $\frac{(-3)^2}{-3}$ (k) $\frac{(-2)^4 \times (-2)^5}{(-2)^3}$ (l) $\frac{(-3)^3 \times (-3)^2}{(-3)^4}$

Assignment 5 Rules

- Use your answers to Exercises 6 and 7 to help you to find rules for simplifying expressions of the type

  $a^x \times a^y$

  and

  $\frac{a^x}{a^y}$

  and

  $(a^x)^y$

- Check your rules work by testing them on some examples of your own.
- Can you find a value for numbers of the form a^0?
  Explain your answer.

Assignment 6 Products

- Look again at the multiplication square you completed in Assignment 1.
- Choose any 2-by-2 square.

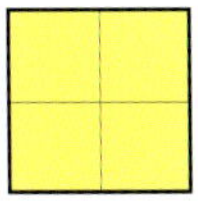

- Write down the product of the four numbers inside the square.
  Which 2-by-2 squares will give the maximum product?
  Which 2-by-2 squares will give the minimum product?
- Write down some more 2-by-2 squares and find the product of the four numbers inside.
- Write down what you notice about the results.
  Explain your answer.

Exercise 8

1 Write down the value of each of these.

(a) 30^2 (b) $\sqrt{144}$ (c) $\sqrt{\left(\frac{1}{25}\right)}$ (d) $\left(\frac{2}{3}\right)^2$

2 Write down the value of each of these cubes.

(a) 4^3 (b) $\left(\frac{1}{2}\right)^3$ (c) $(0.1)^3$ (d) $(0.5)^3$

3 Write down the value of each of these.

(a) $\sqrt[3]{1000}$ (b) $\sqrt[3]{\left(\frac{1}{8}\right)}$ (c) $\frac{\sqrt[3]{8}}{\sqrt[3]{27}}$ (d) $\sqrt[3]{\frac{125}{8}}$

4 Write down the value of each of these.

(a) -4×-1 (b) 6×-2 (c) $8 \div -2$ (d) $-100 \div -2$

(e) $(-5)^2$ (f) 0×-3 (g) $-35 \div 7$ (h) $(-8)^2 \times (-2)^2$

5 Write down the value of each of these.

(a) 2^5 (b) 10^4 (c) $3^2 \times 2^4$ (d) $5^3 \times 2^2$

(e) $10^5 \times 4^3$ (f) $\left(\frac{1}{2}\right)^6$ (g) $(-1)^3$ (h) $(-2)^4$

6 Write down the number which must be written instead of each x to make these statements correct?

(a) $3^x = 81$ (b) $5^x = 125$ (c) $\left(\frac{1}{10}\right)^x = \frac{1}{1000000}$

(d) $(-3)^x = 81$ (e) $(-4)^x = -64$ (f) $(-0.2)^x = -0.00032$

7

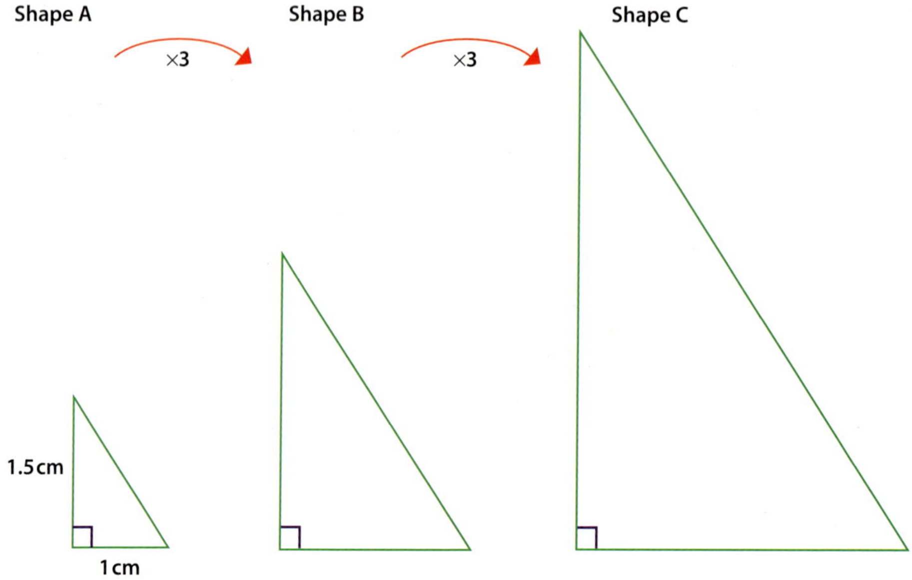

The shape A is repeatedly enlarged by scale factor 3 to produce shapes B, C, D, etc.

(a) Draw shapes B and C and label the sides.

(b) What is the scale factor of the enlargement that would map shape A on to shape E?

8 A child has 64 sweets.

He gives away one quarter of them to his brother and one quarter of those remaining to his sister.

The dog eats one quarter of those left.

(a) Write down how many sweets are eaten by the dog.

(b) What fraction of the child's sweets are eaten by the dog?

9 Write down each of these in a simpler way.

(Do not work out the answer to each calculation.)

(a) $5^3 \times 5^2 \times 5^4$ (b) $((10)^4)^2$ (c) $(-2)^2 \times (-2)^3$

(d) $\frac{3^4}{3^2}$ (e) $\frac{(5^8 \times 5^2)}{5^6}$ (f) $\frac{(3^4 \times 3^2)}{3^3}$

(g) $\frac{(-5)^3}{(-5)^2}$ (h) $\frac{(2^3 \times 2^4 \times 3^4)}{(2^2 \times 3^2)}$ (i) $\frac{(3^4 \times 3^6 \times 5^4)}{(5^2 \times 3^2)}$

10 Using a calculator, find the quickest method for finding the value of each of these expressions.

(a) 12^3 (b) $\sqrt[3]{4913}$ (c) 8^5

(d) $(0.2)^3 \times 5$ (e) $(-6)^4$ (f) $\sqrt[3]{-729}$

(g) 16^4 (h) $(1.5)^4 \times 5$ (i) $12^3 - (-6)^4$

> **A prime factor is a factor which is also a prime number.**

Assignment 7 Prime factors

A factor tree can be used to express a number as a product of its prime factors.

For example

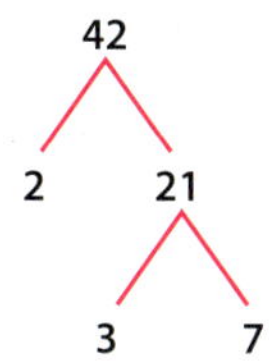

$$42 = 2 \times 21$$
$$= 2 \times 3 \times 7$$

- Draw a factor tree for 30 and use it to help you to write 30 as a product of its prime factors.
- Draw a factor tree for 72 and write down 72 as a product of its prime factors. Try to write your answer in the simplest possible way using powers.
- Use factor trees to express 20 and 24 as a product of their prime factors.
- Write down the highest common factor (HCF) of 20 and 24. Explain how to get this answer from your factor trees for 20 and 24.
- Write down the lowest common multiple of 20 and 24. Explain how to get this answer from your factor trees for 20 and 24.

Assignment 8 Powers of eleven

1

1 1

1 2 1

1 3 3 1

1 4 6 4 1

This triangle is known as Pascal's Triangle, named after the French mathematician Blaise Pascal.

- Copy this triangle and write another four rows for it.
- Write down the values of 11^1, 11^2, 11^3 and 11^4. Look for these values in the triangle and write down what you notice.
- Write down the value of 11^5 and explain how to get this value from the triangle.
- Use the triangle to help you to write down 11^6. Check your answer with a calculator.
- Use a similar method to find 11^7 and 11^8.

Further algebra

In this chapter you will learn:

- → **how to find factors in algebra**
- → **how to change the subject of an equation.**

Starting points

Before starting this chapter, you will need to remember how to:

- find factors of numbers
- work with negative numbers
- expand brackets
- simplify algebraic expressions.

Exercise 1

1 (a) Write down all the factors of each of these numbers.

(i) 24 (ii) 42 (iii) 18
(iv) 36 (v) 29 (vi) 100
(vii) 25 (viii) 120 (ix) 37
(x) 85 (xi) 144 (xii) 111

(b) Write down the numbers in part (a) which are prime numbers.
Describe how the number of factors helps you to find the prime numbers.

(c) Write down the numbers in part (a) which are square numbers.
Explain how you know.

Common factors are factors of both numbers.

2 Write down all the common factors of each of these pairs of numbers.

(a) 12, 18 (b) 25, 15 (c) 10, 20
(d) 24, 60 (e) 78, 195 (f) 24, 84
(g) 170, 34 (h) 38, 57 (i) 399, 357

3 Work out the value of each of these expressions.

(a) $3(2+1)$ (b) $3-(2+1)$ (c) $3(2-1)$
(d) $\frac{6}{2+1}$ (e) $\frac{10-4}{3}$ (f) $\frac{8-4}{2}+1$

4 Write down the value of each of these expressions.

(a) $4+(-2)$ (b) $(-3)\times 5$ (c) $(-4)+(-7)$
(d) $(-6)-4$ (e) $(-6)\times(-7)$ (f) $4-(-6)$
(g) $15\div(-5)$ (h) $(-8)-(-6)$ (i) $(-12)\div(-3)$
(j) $2(3+(-4))$ (k) $-4(-5-(-3))$ (l) $-5(5-(-5)-(-5))$

5 (a) Copy each of these equations and complete them by inserting brackets to make each one correct. Use as few brackets as possible.

(i) $3 + 2 \times 5 - 4 = 5$ (ii) $3 + 2 \times 5 - 4 = 21$

(iii) $3 + 2 \times 5 - 4 = 9$ (iv) $8 - 4 + 6 \div 2 = 7$

(v) $8 - 4 + 6 \div 2 = 3$ (vi) $8 - 4 + 6 \div 2 = 1$

(b) Find as many different values as possible for $8 + 5 \times 4 - 7$ by inserting brackets in different positions.

6 Write each of these expressions as simply as possible.

(a) $a + a + a + b + b$ (b) $p + q + p + p + q + p$ (c) $s + t - s + t$

(d) $2m - n + 3m + 4n$ (e) $2w - 3t - w + 4t$ (f) $3x + 2y + 2x - 4z - x - 3z$

Multiplying algebraic expressions

Examples

$2(x + y)$

	x	$+y$
2	$2x$	$+2y$

$2(x + y) = 2x + 2y$

$-3(x - 2y)$

	x	$-2y$
-3	$-3x$	$+6y$

$-3(x - 2y) = -3x + 6y$

$(x + 2)(x + 1)$

	x	$+1$
x	x^2	$+1x$
$+2$	$+2x$	$+2$

$$(x + 2)(x + 1) = x^2 + 1x + 2x + 2$$
$$= x^2 + 3x + 2$$

Exercise 2

1 For each of these expressions, write down an equivalent expression without brackets.

(a) $2(a + b)$ (b) $4(s - t)$ (c) $3(p + 2q)$ (d) $2(3m + 5n)$

(e) $4(2v - 3t)$ (f) $f(g + h)$ (g) $w(3t - d)$ (h) $2e(k + h)$

(i) $3m(2f - g)$ (j) $d(3d - 2e)$ (k) $a^2(a + b)$ (l) $2s^2(2k - 4s)$

2 For each of these expressions, write down an equivalent expression without brackets. Write your answer as simply as possible.

(a) $2(a + b) + 3(a + b)$ (b) $2(p + 3q) + (p + q)$

(c) $4(a + 3b) + 2(2a + b)$ (d) $3(c + d) + 2(c - d)$

(e) $5(2s + 3t) + 4(3s - 2t)$ (f) $2(p - q) + 3(2p - 4q)$

(g) $4(x + y) - 3(x + y)$ (h) $2(3t + 2p) - 3(2t + p)$

(i) $4(2d - 3e) - 2(3d + 2e)$ (j) $5(3a + 2b) - 2(2a - b)$

(k) $4(3d + 3e) - 3(2d - 4e)$ (l) $2(2f - 3g) - 3(f - 2g)$

3 For each of these expressions, write down an equivalent expression without brackets.

Write your answer as simply as possible.

(a) $(a+2)(a+3)$ (b) $(c+4)(c+2)$

(c) $(p+5)(p+5)$ (d) $(m+5)(m-3)$

(e) $(2p+4)(p+2)$ (f) $(3x+4)(2x+2)$

(g) $(2f+4)(3f-2)$ (h) $(p-3)(p-2)$

(i) $(3g-4)(2g-5)$ (j) $(a+b)(a+b)$

(k) $(a+b)(a-b)$ (l) $(2s-t)(s-2t)$

$(x+1)(x+2)$

	x	$+1$
x	x^2	$+1x$
$+2$	$+2x$	$+2$

$x^2+1x+2x+2$
$=x^2+3x+2$

Factorising

Key fact

Factorise means rewrite with brackets, with a factor of the expression written outside the brackets as a multiplier.

Exercise 3

1 The factors of $6r^2$ are 1, 2, 3, 6, r, $2r$, $3r$, $6r$, r^2, $2r^2$, $3r^2$, $6r^2$.

Write down all the factors of each of these expressions.

(a) $2c$ (b) $3a$ (c) $6d$ (d) $2bc$

(e) $12fg$ (f) a^2 (g) $3m^2$ (h) $8s^2$

(i) ab^2 (j) $6f^2g$ (k) $16t^3$ (l) $3de^2f$

2 Write down all the common factors of each of these pairs of expressions.

(a) $2a$, $4b$ (b) $2a$, $5a$ (c) 3, $6d$ (d) $12c$, $4e$

(e) $6p$, $8p$ (f) mn, $2m$ (g) $6fg$, $4gh$ (h) $8g^2$, $10gh$

(i) x^2, $2xy$ (j) $2t$, $6t^2$ (k) $2t^3$, s^2t^2 (l) $3ab^2$, $3a^2b$

The highest common factor is the largest factor of both expressions.

3 Write down the highest common factor of each of these pairs of expressions.

(a) $2a$, $4b$ (b) $4x$, $6y$ (c) $3d$, $4d$ (d) $6a$, $4a$

(e) $4pq$, $8q$ (f) $2st$, $8st$ (g) $15r$, $10rs$ (h) $9ab$, $3b$

(i) a^3, $2a^2$ (j) $3b^3$, $6b^2$ (k) $4jk$, $6k^2z$ (l) $10pq^2$, $16p^2q$

4 Copy these expressions.

$2x+4$ $2(x+4)$ $\frac{2x+12}{2}$

$\frac{9x+6}{3}$ $4x+2$ $6x-4$

$3(x+2)$ $\frac{1}{2}(4x+8)$ $2(x+2)$

(a) Cross out all the expressions that do *not* have the value 8 when $x=2$

(b) Cross out all of the remaining expressions that do *not* have the value 14 when $x=5$.

(c) Explain why all the expressions you have not crossed out are equivalent to each other.

5 Copy these diagrams and complete them by writing an expression in each shaded region.

(a)

	$x + 2$
2	$2x + 4$

$2(x + 2) =$

(b)

	$x + 2$
	$3x + 6$

$= 3x + 6$

(c)

	$2x + 3$
	$8x + 12$

$= 8x + 12$

(d)

3	$6x + 3$

$= 6x + 3$

(e)

2	$4x - 6$

$= 4x - 6$

(f)

	$6x - 4$

$= 6x - 4$

6 Copy and complete each of these by rewriting the expression using brackets. Choose the largest number possible outside the brackets. The first one has been done for you.

(a) $3x + 6 = 3(x + 2)$ (b) $2x + 4 =$ (c) $4a + 8 =$

(d) $4d + 6 =$ (e) $12g + 8 =$ (f) $3a - 9 =$

(g) $8m - 6 =$ (h) $8 - 4m =$ (i) $10 - 5t =$

7 Copy these diagrams and complete them by writing an expression in each shaded region.

(a)

	$x + 3$
x	$x^2 + 3x$

$x(x + 3) =$

(b)

x	$x^2 + 5x$

$= x^2 + 5x$

(c)

	$x^2 - 2x$

$= x^2 - 2x$

(d)

	$3a + 2a^2$

$= 3a + 2a^2$

(e)

	$4p + 6p^2$

$= 4p + 6p^2$

(f)

	$3t^2 - 9t$

$= 3t^2 - 9t$

8 Factorise these expressions. The first one has been done for you.

(a) $5a + 10 = 5(a + 2)$ (b) $4a + 2$ (c) $3a + ab$

(d) $a^2 + 2a$ (e) $2b^2 + 4b$ (f) $3b + 9b^2$

(g) $2x^2 - x$ (h) $ax - 2x^2$ (i) $ab - ab^2$

(j) $x^2y + xy^2$ (k) $2mn - 4n^2$ (l) $pq^3 - 2p^2q$

Factorising an expression means rewriting it with any common factors shown outside a bracket.

Assignment 1 Multiplication grids

You are familiar with a multiplication square that looks like this:

1	2	3	4	5	6	7	8	9	10
2	4	6	8	10	12	14	16	18	20
3	6	9	12	15	18	21	24	27	30
4	8	12	16	20	24	28	32	36	40
5	10	15	20	25	30	35	40	45	50
6	12	18	24	30	36	42	48	54	60
7	14	21	28	35	42	49	56	63	70
8	16	24	32	40	48	56	64	72	80
9	18	27	36	45	54	63	72	81	90
10	20	30	40	50	60	70	80	90	100

This smaller grid lies within the multiplication square.

12	15	18	21	24	27
16	20	24	28	32	36
20	25	30	35	40	45
24	30	36	42	48	54
28	35	42	49	56	63
32	40	48	56	64	72

Letting $a = 12$, the numbers in grid could be rewritten as algebraic expressions. For example,

a	$a+3$	$a+6$	$a+9$	$2a$	$2a+3$
$a+4$	$a+8$	$2a$	$2(a+2)$	$2(a+4)$	
$a+8$	$2a+1$	$2(a+3)$	$2a+11$		
$2a$	$2(a+3)$	$3a$			
$2(a+2)$	$2a+11$				
$2(a+4)$	$3a+4$	$4a$			

- Copy and complete this grid, writing a correct algebraic expression in each cell.

- A 4-by-4 grid is selected from the multiplication square. This time $a = 6$. Use this information to identify the square and complete the grid.

a			$a + 9$
$2a$			$2(a + 9)$

- In a 5-by-6 grid, the value of a is 24. Use this information to identify the grid's position within the multiplication square.

$a - 20$					a
					$2a$

- Copy the grid and write a correct algebraic expression in at least three more cells.

Exercise 4

1 Use the information given in this grid to locate where the grid fits within the multiplication square and so find the value of a.

a			$a + 15$
$2a$		$2(a + 10)$	

2 Repeat Question 1 using this grid.

$\frac{a}{4}$					
		$a - 24$			a

Assignment 2 Algebraic grids

In this grid, the value of a is 24. You identified its position within the grid in Assignment 1.

$a - 20$					a
					$2a$

- For each of the two shaded boxes, write an algebraic expression which describes the number that appears in that position within the multiplication grid.
- Simplify your expressions as much as possible.

Exercise 5

1 In Question 1 of Exercise 4, you located the position of this grid within the multiplication grid, and decided on a value for a.

	a			$a + 15$
	$2a$		$2(a + 10)$	

Write expressions using the letter a which describe the shaded squares on the grid. Simplify your expressions as much as possible.

2 Part of this grid appeared in Question 2 of Exercise 4.

$\frac{a}{4}$					
		$a - 24$			a

Write expressions using the letter a which describe the shaded squares on the grid. Simplify your expressions as much as possible.

Finding the factors of algebraic expressions

Exercise 6

1 Copy these diagrams and complete them.
The first one has been done for you.

(a)

	x	$+4$
x	x^2	$+4x$
$+2$	$+2x$	$+8$

$x^2 + 6x + 8 = (x + 2)(x + 4)$

(b)

	x	$+4$
	x^2	$+4x$
	$+1x$	$+4$

$x^2 + 5x + 4 = (\quad)(\quad)$

(c)

	x	$+5$
	x^2	$+5x$
	$+2x$	$+10$

$= (\quad)(\quad)$

(d)

	x	-4
	x^2	$-4x$
	$+2x$	-8

$= (\quad)(\quad)$

2 Copy these statements and complete them using a grid like the ones used in Question 1.

(a) $x^2 + 2x + 1 = (x + 1)(x + \quad)$
(b) $x^2 + 3x + 2 = (x + 2)(\quad)$
(c) $x^2 + 6x + 9 = (x + 3)(\quad)$
(d) $x^2 + \quad x - 2 = (x + 2)(\quad)$
(e) $x^2 - \quad x - 6 = (x + 2)(\quad)$
(f) $x^2 - 2x + 1 = (x - 1)(\quad)$

> Look for pairs of numbers which multiply together to make the constant term and add together to make the coefficent of *x*.

3 Factorise these expressions.
The first one has been done for you.

(a) $x^2 + 5x + 4 = (x + 1)(x + 4)$
(b) $x^2 + 5x + 6$
(c) $x^2 + 4x + 4$
(d) $x^2 + 7x + 6$
(e) $x^2 + \quad x - 6$
(f) $x^2 + \quad x - 12$
(g) $x^2 - 3x + 2$
(h) $x^2 - 3x - 10$

4 Write these fractions as simply as possible.
You may find that it helps to factorise the expression on the top of the fraction.
Show all your working.

(a) $\frac{4c}{2}$
(b) $\frac{ab}{a}$
(c) $\frac{4g}{2g}$
(d) $\frac{9h}{3}$
(e) $\frac{4d + 2}{2}$
(f) $\frac{g^2 + 2g}{g}$
(g) $\frac{p^2 + 3p + 2}{p + 2}$
(h) $\frac{t^2 + 5t + 6}{t + 3}$

Dividing with algebraic terms

You have probably seen long division sums written like this.

$$\begin{array}{r}
23 \\
12\overline{)276} \\
\underline{24} \\
36 \\
\underline{36} \\
00
\end{array}$$

Look carefully at this alternative. Make sure you understand how it has been carried out before you move on.

$$\begin{array}{rl}
20 + 3 & \\
10 + 2\ \overline{)200 + 70 + 6} & \\
\underline{200 + 40} & (10 \times 20) + (2 \times 20) = 200 + 40 \\
30 + 6 & \\
\underline{30 + 6} & (10 \times 3) + (2 \times 3) = 30 + 6 \\
0 + 0 &
\end{array}$$

A number can be divided by its factors without leaving a remainder.

An algebraic expression can also be divided by its factors.

$(x + 1)$ is a factor of $2x^2 + 5x + 3$. The division can be carried out like this.

$$\begin{array}{rl}
2x + 3 & \\
x + 1\ \overline{)2x^2 + 5x + 3} & \\
\underline{2x^2 + 2x} & (x \times 2x) + (1 \times 2x) = 2x^2 + 2x \\
3x + 3 & \\
\underline{3x + 3} & (x \times 3) + (1 \times 3) = 3x + 3 \\
0 &
\end{array}$$

Exercise 7

1 Divide these expressions by the factor given.

(a) $x^2 + 3x + 2$, factor $(x + 1)$

(b) $x^2 + 5x + 6$, factor $(x + 3)$

(c) $x^2 + x - 2$, factor $(x + 2)$

(d) $x^2 - 5x + 6$, factor $(x - 2)$

(e) $2x^2 + 3x + 1$, factor $(2x + 1)$

(f) $3x^2 + 5x + 2$, factor $(x + 1)$

(g) $4x^2 + 4x + 1$, factor $(2x + 1)$

(h) $4x^2 + 8x + 3$, factor $(2x + 1)$

2 Multiply your answer to each part of Question 1 by the factor given to check your answers are correct.

Changing the subject

Sometimes it is necessary to make a different letter the subject of an equation.

Example

$h = k + 2$

Here, h is the subject.

[–2] $h - 2 = k + 2 - 2$

$h - 2 = k$

$k = h - 2$

The equation has been changed to make k the subject.

Example

$x = \frac{y + 2}{3}$

Here, x is the subject.

[×3] $3x = y + 2$

[–2] $3x - 2 = y + 2 - 2$

$3x - 2 = y$

$y = 3x - 2$

The equation now has y as the subject.

[×3] is shorthand for 'multiply both sides by 3'.

Exercise 8

Answers can be checked by replacing letters with numbers.

1 Make s the subject of each of these equations.

(a) $t = s + 3$ (b) $t = s + \frac{1}{4}$ (c) $t = s - 6$

(d) $t = s - \frac{1}{2}$ (e) $t = 2s$ (f) $t = 3s$

(g) $t = \frac{1}{2}s$ (h) $t = \frac{s}{3}$ (i) $3t = 4s$

2 Make n the subject of each of these equations.

(a) $m = 2n + 1$ (b) $m = 2(n + 1)$ (c) $m = 3(n - 2)$

(d) $m = 3n - 2$ (e) $m = \frac{1}{2}n + 2$ (f) $m = \frac{1}{2}(n + 2)$

(g) $m = \frac{n + 3}{2}$ (h) $m = \frac{n - 4}{3}$ (i) $m = \frac{1}{2}n + 5$

3 Write these equations with s as the subject.

(a) $r = s + t$ (b) $r = st$ (c) $r = st + 3$

(d) $r = \frac{s}{t}$ (e) $r = \frac{s}{t} + 2$ (f) $r = \frac{t + 2}{s}$

(g) $r = s - at$ (h) $r = \frac{at}{s}$ (i) $r = \frac{at - 2}{s}$

4 Repeat Question 3, this time making t the subject of each equation.

5 Make b the subject of these equations.

(a) $a = \frac{1}{3}(b + 4)$ (b) $a = \frac{1}{4}b + 2$ (c) $a = \frac{1}{2}(3b + 5)$

(d) $a = \frac{1}{5}b - 2$ (e) $a = \frac{1}{4}(3b - 3)$ (f) $a = \frac{1}{4}(3b + 1)$

(g) $a = \frac{2b + 1}{3}$ (h) $a = \frac{3}{4}(b + 2)$ (i) $a = \frac{2b - 3}{5}$

6 The equation $C = 2\pi r$ is used to calculate the circumference (C) of a circle using the radius (r).

Change the subject of this equation to give an equation to calculate the radius (r) if you know the circumference (C).

7 The equation $A = \pi r^2$ is used to calculate the area (A) of a circle using the radius (r). Change the subject of the equation to give an equation to calculate the radius (r) if you know the area (A).

8 Pythagoras' Theorem says that, for any right-angled triangle, the lengths of the sides are linked by this equation:

$a^2 = b^2 + c^2$

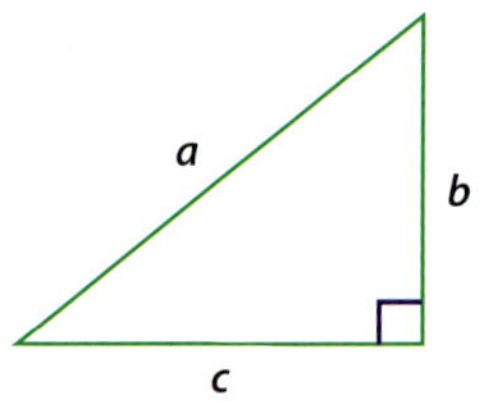

Write down an equation which can be used to calculate the length of the side labelled b.

9 Make t the subject of each of these equations.

(a) $d = t^2$ (b) $d = \sqrt{t}$ (c) $d = t^2 + 2$

(d) $d = \sqrt{t - 3}$ (e) $d = \sqrt{t} + 4$ (f) $d = (t + 2)^2$

(g) $d = (3t)^2$ (h) $d = \sqrt{4t - 3}$ (i) $d = (5t + 4)^2$

10 Create as many different equations as possible by changing the subject in each of these equations.

(a) $v = u + at$ (b) $a = b^2 + c$ (c) $m = \frac{p - q}{r}$

(d) $p = \sqrt{\frac{q - 2r}{s}}$ (e) $a = b^2 + cd$ (f) $a = \frac{v^2 - u^2}{2s}$

Exercise 9

1 Write down all the factors of these expressions.

(a) $4p$ (b) $12p^2$ (c) pq

(d) $6pq$ (e) $8p^2q$ (f) $6p^2q^2$

2 Write down all the common factors of these pairs of expressions.

(a) $2p, 4q$ (b) $3p, 5p$ (c) $4pq, 6qr$

(d) $3p^2q, 6q$ (e) $4pqr, 6p^2r^2$ (f) $2p + 4q, 6pq$

3 Copy and complete these equations.

(a) $4d + 6 = 2(\quad)$ (b) $3b + 5b^2 = b(\quad)$

(c) $6 - 4g = \quad(3 - 2g)$ (d) $6b^2 - 3b = \quad(2b - 1)$

(e) $2h - 4h^2 = 2h(\quad)$ (f) $ah - bh = \quad(a - b)$

4 Factorise these expressions.

(a) $5w + 10$ (b) $a^2 + a$ (c) $4a + 6b$ (d) $9f - 3$

(e) $4p^2 - 2p$ (f) $ab + bc$ (g) $2ab - 4bc$ (h) $3cd + 6de$

5 Copy these diagrams and complete them.

(a)

	x	$+4$
	x^2	$+4x$
	$+3x$	$+12$

$x^2 + 7x + 12 = (\quad)(\quad)$

(b)

	x	-3
	x^2	$-3x$
	$+2x$	-6

$x^2 - x - 6 = (\quad)(\quad)$

(c)

	x	
	x^2	$+2x$
	$+5x$	$+10$

$x^2 + 7x + 10 = (\quad)(\quad)$

(d)

	x^2	$-2x$
	$-3x$	$+6$

$x^2 - 5x + 6 = (\quad)(\quad)$

(e)

	x^2	
	$-5x$	-10

$= (\quad)(\quad)$

(f)

	x^2	
		$+7$

$= (\quad)(\quad)$

6 Factorise these expressions.

(a) $b^2 + 3b + 2$ (b) $t^2 - 6t + 8$ (c) $x^2 - 2x - 15$ (d) $p^2 + 7p - 8$

7 Make d the subject of these equations.

(a) $a = 2d - 3$ (b) $m = 3(d - 4)$ (c) $b = 4d + 3$ (d) $p = 5(d + 3)$

(e) $t = \frac{1}{2}(d - 3)$ (f) $k = \frac{d}{3} - 2$ (g) $h = \frac{d + 3}{5}$ (h) $y = \frac{ad}{c}$

(i) $u = ad + c$ (j) $r = 3d - w$ (k) $st = \sqrt{d}$ (l) $a + b = d^2$

8 Write down as many different equations as you can by changing the subject or factorising these two equations.

(a) $2a + 4 = 6b^2 + 4b$ (b) $\frac{p^2 - 3p}{q} = 2(q - p)$

Pythagoras and proof

In this chapter you will learn:

- ➜ **about using Pythagoras' Theorem in harder problems in 2D**
- ➜ **about using Pythagoras' Theorem in 3D problems**
- ➜ **the difference between illustration and proof**
- ➜ **more about Pythagorean triples.**

Starting points

Before starting this chapter, you will need to use Pythagoras' Theorem:

- to find the length of a hypotenuse
- to find the length of shorter sides of a triangle.

Assignment 1 A cross square

- Make a copy of this cross.

- Cut the cross into four pieces and use the pieces to make a square.

Exercise 1

1 Use Pythagoras' Theorem to calculate the lengths marked a and b in these two triangles.

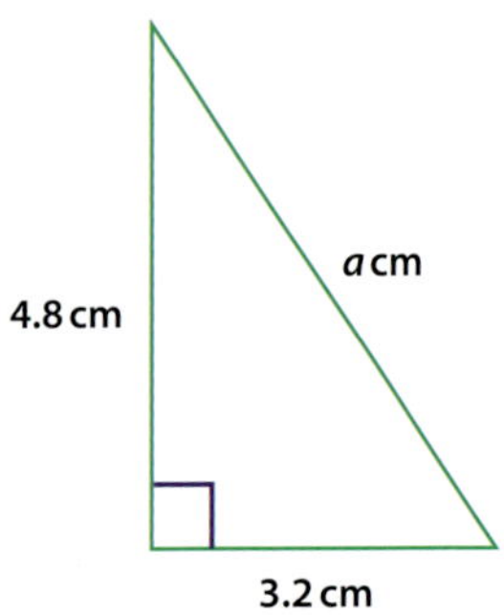

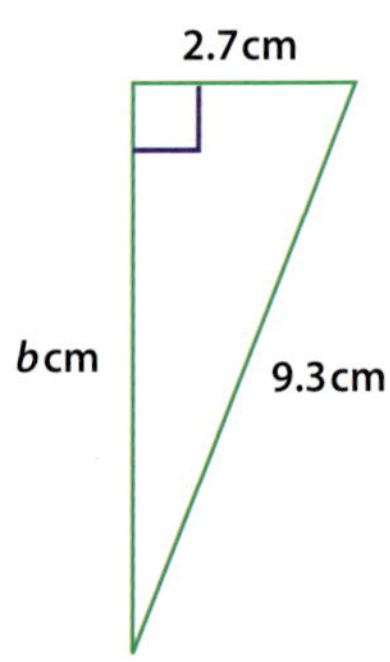

Key fact

Pythagoras' Theorem

In a right-angled triangle, the square on the hypotenuse is equal in area to the sum of the squares on the other two sides.

2 What is the value of *c*?

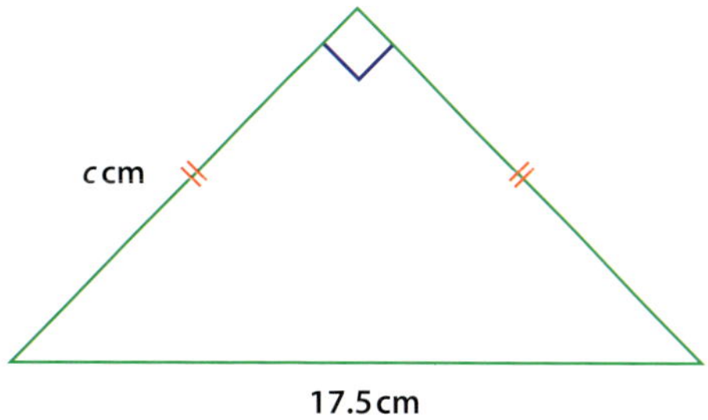

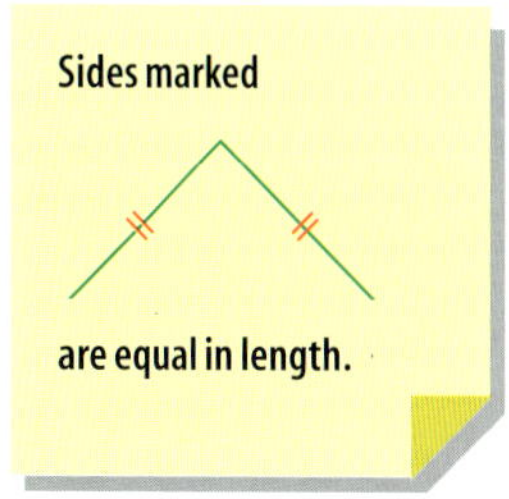

3 In this diagram, $x = 3.5$. What is the value of *d*?

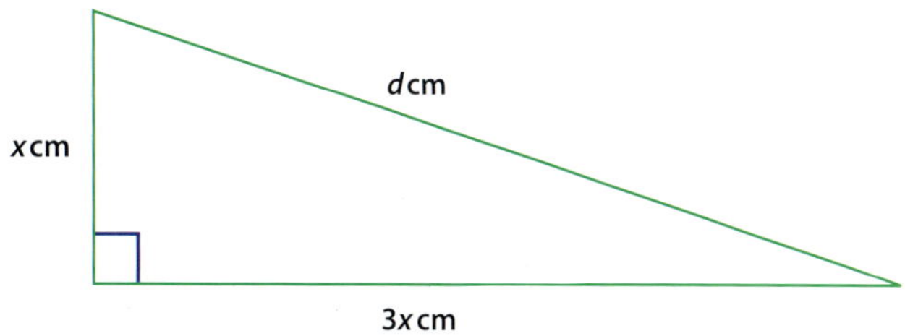

4 In this diagram, the length of AC is twice that of AB. What is the value of *e*?

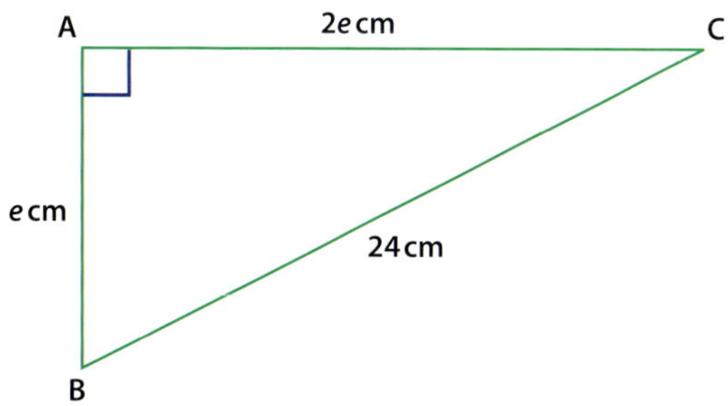

Using Pythagoras' Theorem

Pythagoras' Theorem can be applied to any right-angled triangle.

Other shapes may be divided into right-angled triangles, so the theorem may be helpful for many problems. It is always worth looking for such triangles.

When solving problems involving triangles, remember:

- to draw clear diagrams
- to look at the information carefully
- to look for right-angled triangles; if necessary add construction lines to create them.

Example

A rhombus has diagonals of lengths 12 cm and 9 cm. Find the length of its side.

First, draw a clear diagram.

> **The diagonals of a rhombus bisect at right angles.**

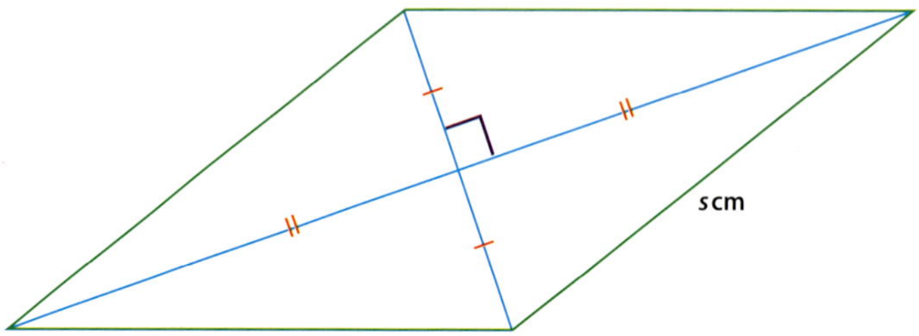

Notice that the shape can be divided into four right-angled triangles.

Consider just one of these.

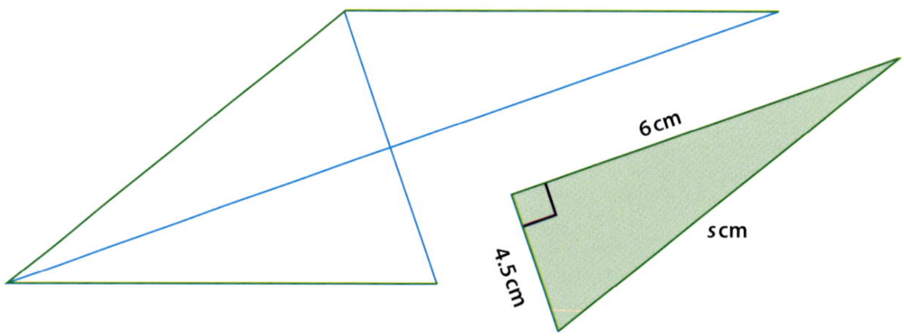

Use Pythagoras' Theorem to find the side length, s cm:

$$\begin{aligned} s^2 &= 6^2 + 4.5^2 \\ &= 36 + 20.25 \\ &= 56.25 \\ s &= \sqrt{56.25} \\ &= 7.5 \end{aligned}$$

So, the length of the side of the rhombus is 7.5 cm.

Exercise 2

1 Find the lengths of the sides marked a to f in the diagrams below.

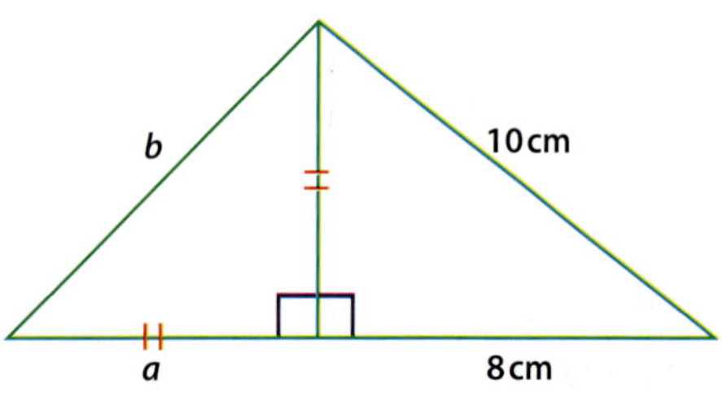

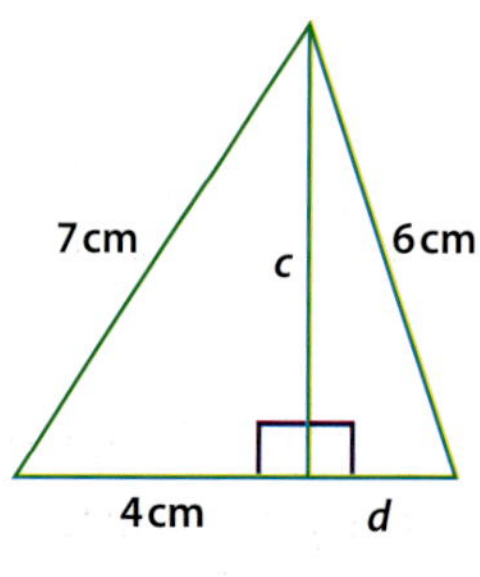

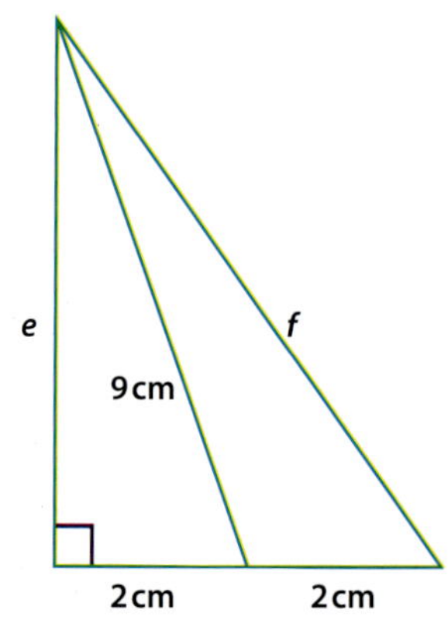

2 Find the length of the line AB.

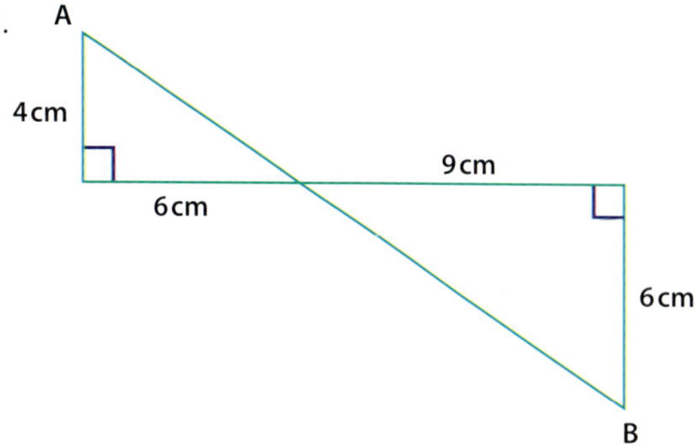

3 Find the lengths of the sides marked a and b.

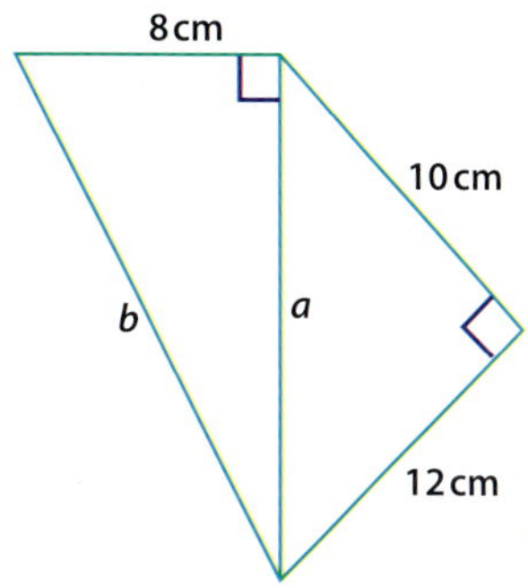

4 Two radio masts are 55 metres apart. A wire is stretched tightly between the tops of the masts. If one mast is 50 m tall and the other is 60 m tall, what is the length of the wire?

5 A ladder is 7 metres long. It is placed so that its foot is 2.5 m from a wall. How far up the wall will the ladder reach?

6 A rhombus has sides of length 7 cm. Its shorter diagonal is 4 cm long. How long is the other diagonal?

7 Triangle ABC has a right angle at A. The length of side AB is twice that of side AC. If the length of side AC is b cm:

(a) what is length of side AB in terms of b?

(b) what is length of side BC in terms of b?

8 Triangle ABC has a right angle at A.

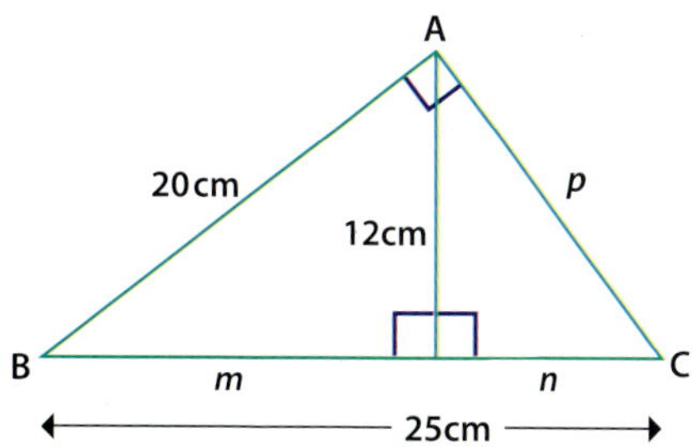

(a) Calculate the length of the side labelled m.

(b) Calculate the length of the side labelled n.

(c) Calculate the length of the side labelled p.

3D challenges!

Exercise 3

1 A box is made in the shape of a cube. Its dimensions are of length 8 cm.

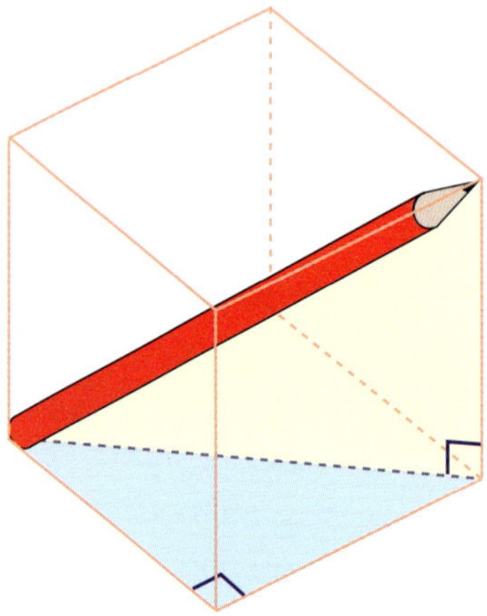

What is the length of the longest pencil that would fit inside the box?

2 A room is 2.3 m high, 4 m long and 3 m wide.

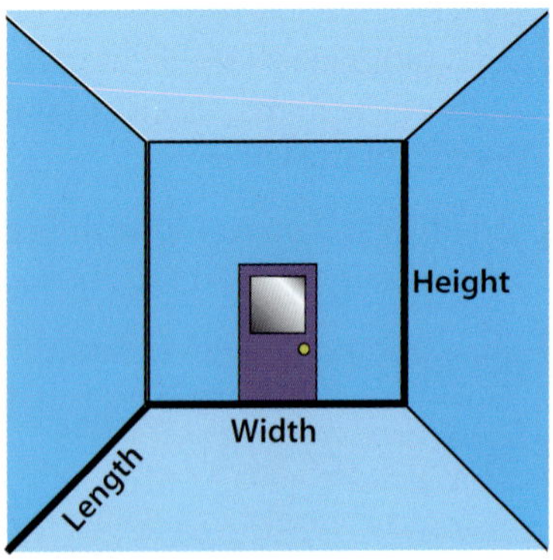

Find the shortest distance from one corner of the room at floor level to the diagonally opposite corner at ceiling level.

Try to picture each problem in your head.

3 A fish tank has dimensions of 30 cm, 50 cm and 90 cm. A stick reaches from one corner at the bottom to the opposite corner at the top.
What is the length of the stick?

4 A shoe box measures 35 cm by 15 cm by 15 cm.
What is the shortest distance between diagonally opposite corners?

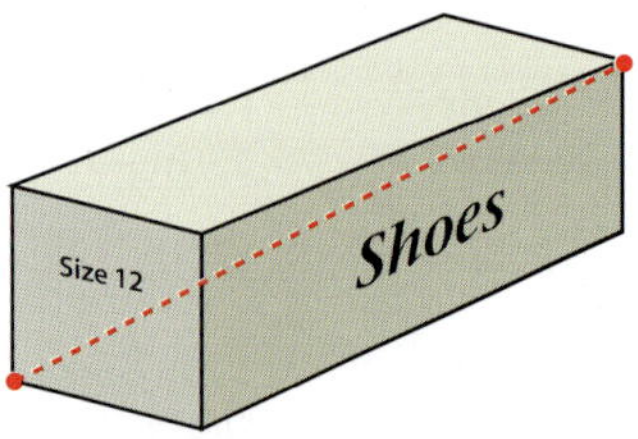

Draw a clear diagram for each situation.

Look for right angles.

5 A rectangular box has dimensions of 3 cm, 6 cm and 10 cm.
What is the length of the longest diagonal of the box?

6 A rectangular box has dimensions of a cm, b cm and c cm.
Find an expression for the length of the interior diagonal of the box.

7 A square-based box has an interior diagonal of 30 cm.
If the height of the box is twice the length of a base side, find the box's dimensions.

Hint: Use your answer to Question 6 to form an equation. Solve by trial and improvement.

8 A square-based pyramid has a height of 10 cm. Its top is immediately above the centre of the base. Its base has sides of 12 cm.

(a) Draw a diagram of the pyramid, recording the lengths clearly.

(b) Calculate the perpendicular height of one of the triangular faces.

(c) Calculate the length of one of the sloping edges.

Illustration versus proof

There are over 370 recorded different proofs of Pythagoras' Theorem. You met many illustrations of this particular theorem in Chapter 8 of Book 3, but illustrations are not the same as proofs.

To demonstrate the difference between an illustration and a proof, consider this statement:

The result of adding an odd number to an even number is always an odd number.

This statement is easy to test, or demonstrate. Try some examples:

An odd number	An even number	Add them	Result
7	8	7 + 8 = 15	15 is an odd number
23	100	23 + 100 = 123	123 is an odd number
1	72	1 + 72 = 73	73 is an odd number

It works for these three examples. The results show that the statement is true for these three examples, but do not prove it for *all* possible odd and even numbers.

Just looking at examples is illustrating the statement, but it is *not* proving it to be true. To disprove it, all you need to do is to find one example that does not work.

In mathematics you have to be sure that a statement works for *every* possible example before knowing that it is true.

However, algebra can be used to prove the statement.

Proof

First, to prove the statement for *all* examples, we need to generalise.

Consider two numbers: m and n.

Every even number can be described as double (i.e. 2 times) some other number.

$2m$ and $2n$ are even numbers.

Every odd number can be described as one less than an even number.

$2n - 1$ is an odd number.

Adding the odd number to the even number gives:

$2m + 2n - 1$

$= 2(m + n) - 1$

Whatever m and n are, odd or even, their sum is multiplied by 2 which makes an even number. So, $2(m + n)$ is an even number.

Now, $2(m + n) - 1$ is 1 different from an even number, so it must be an odd number.

Because m and n are *any* numbers, the statement is proved for *all* numbers.

Assignment 2 Odd add odd

- Prove this statement:

  An odd number added to another odd number always gives an even result.

odd + odd = even?

Proving Pythagoras' Theorem

Pythagoras proved his theorem using similar triangles. See if you can follow his argument.

Look at this right-angled triangle, ABC, with a perpendicular drawn from the point C on to AB, meeting AB at the point D.

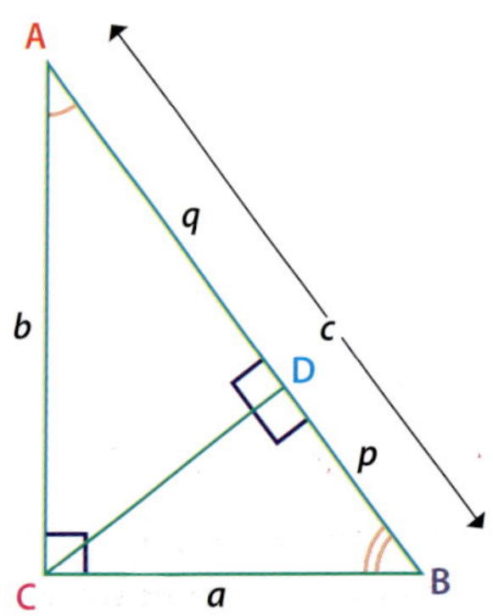

Notice that the main triangle is divided into two smaller right-angled triangles.

We need to prove that:

$a^2 + b^2 = c^2$

Here are all three triangles drawn separately.

All three triangles have a right angle.

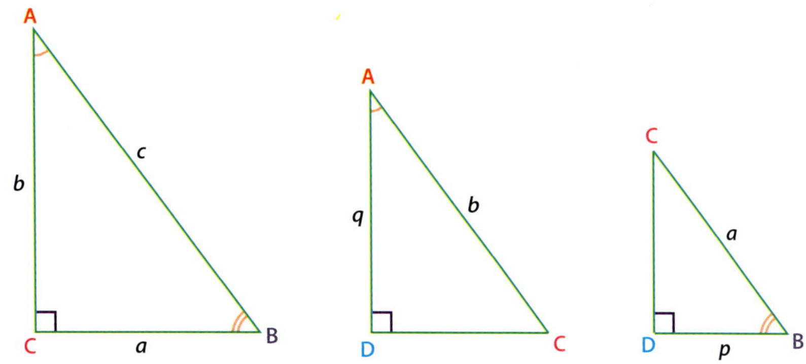

Looking at triangles ACD and ABC, notice that

$\angle DAC = \angle CAB$

so

$\angle DCA = \angle CBA$

Looking at triangles BCD and ABC, notice that

$\angle CBA = \angle DBC$

and so

$\angle CAB = \angle DCB$

Therefore all three triangles have the same three angles and thus are similar.

In similar shapes or triangles, the ratio of corresponding sides is the same.

Looking at triangles ABC and BCD

$$\frac{c}{a} = \frac{a}{p}$$

Multiplying both sides of this equation by ap (to get rid of the fractions) gives:

$$ap \times \frac{c}{a} = ap \times \frac{a}{p}$$

$$cp = a^2$$

Looking at triangles ABC and ACD in the same way gives

$$\frac{c}{b} = \frac{b}{q}$$

Multiplying both sides of this equation by bq gives

$$bq \times \frac{c}{b} = bq \times \frac{b}{q}$$

$$cq = b^2$$

We now use these two equations to find an expression for a^2 and b^2.

$$a^2 + b^2 = cp + cq$$

$$= c(p + q)$$

But $p + q = c$, so we have proved that

$$a^2 + b^2 = c^2$$

Notice that because a, b, c, p and q were general values, and work for any right-angled triangle, we have proved Pythagoras' Theorem for all right-angled triangles.

Assignment 3 A dotty proof for Pythagoras

- Using square, dotty paper, draw one of the more unusual squares. Here is an example.

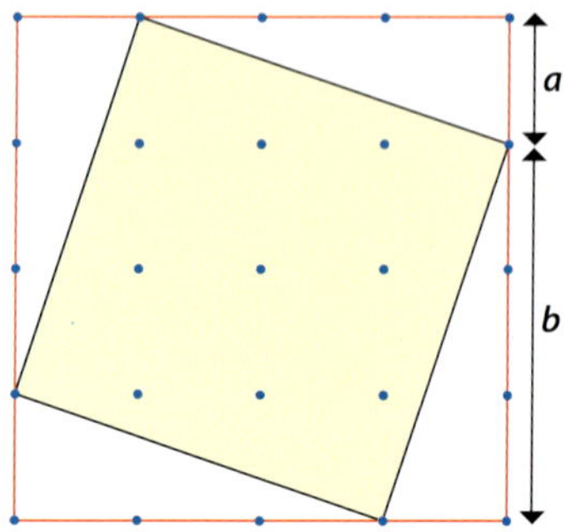

- Use the actual sizes of your diagram to show that the shaded area is $a^2 + b^2$. You may show this by cutting and rearranging.
- Call the side of your square c and try to prove Pythagoras' Theorem using this diagram.

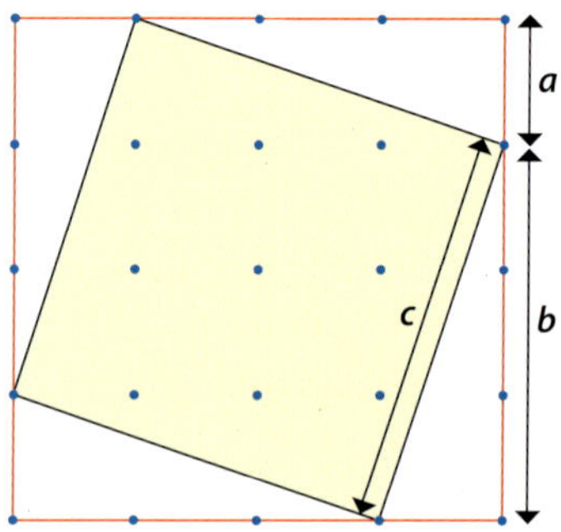

Assignment 4 Garfield's proof for Pythagoras

In 1876, President Garfield, the 20th President of the USA, used the area of a trapezium to prove Pythagoras' Theorem.

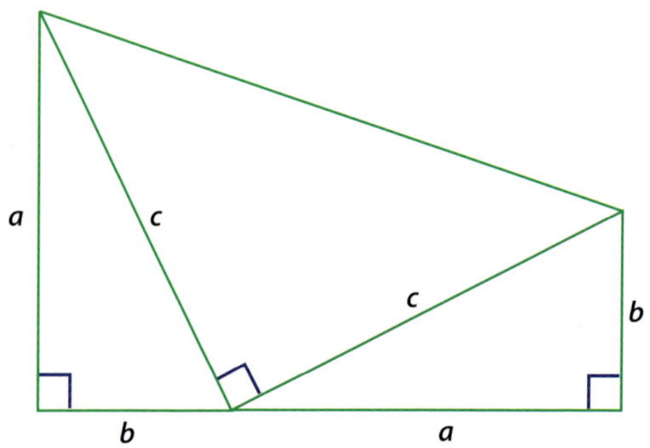

- Prove Pythagoras' Theorem using President Garfield's construction.

Pythagorean triples

Pythagorean triples are numbers such as 3, 4, 5, which obey the rule:

$a^2 + b^2 = c^2$

The numbers must be integers.

An integer is a whole number.

Assignment 5 — Triple search

- Find as many Pythagorean triples as you can. Check to make sure they are correct.

Assignment 6 — Pythagoras multiplied

- Prove that any multiple of the triple 3, 4, 5 is also a Pythagorean triple.

Plato's triples

Plato was one of the first people to find an easier way to collect Pythagorean triples. He generalised the triple into three numbers: $m^2 - 1$, $2m$ and $m^2 + 1$ where m is any integer.

Assignment 7 — Making Plato's triples

- By using each of the first five digits as m, find the first five triples of Plato.
- Compare your triples with Plato's. Can all of your triples be formed from Plato's version?
- Find triples that *cannot* be expressed in Plato's way.
- Prove that Plato's triples will *always* be Pythagorean triples.

Euclid's triples

Euclid later produced a more efficient way of collecting Pythagorean triples. For any two integers s and t, these three numbers form a triple: $s^2 - t^2$, $2st$ and $s^2 + t^2$.

Assignment 8 — Making Euclid's triples

- Fit your triples from Assignment 5 to Euclid's triples.
- Use Euclid's version to generate some more triples.
- Look carefully at all the triples you have found. Which triples contain a multiple of 3, or a multiple of 4, or 5? Comment on your findings.

Fermat's Last Theorem

The equation $a^n + b^n = c^n$ is said to have integer values for a, b, c only when $n = 2$.

This statement, known as Fermat's Last Theorem, remained unproven for many centuries. It was finally proved to be true in 1995.

Comparing data

In this chapter you will learn:

- → **how to find the mean of grouped data**
- → **how to construct a cumulative frequency graph**
- → **how to find the upper and lower quartile**
- → **how to find the interquartile range**
- → **how to construct a box plot.**

Starting points

Before starting this chapter, you will need to know how to:

- calculate the mean, median and range of a set of data
- group data
- draw a frequency polygon.

Exercise 1

1 Here are the heights in centimetres (to the nearest whole number) of seven girls:

162 156 169 160 163 169 173

(a) Calculate the mean height.

(b) Calculate the median height.

(c) Write down the modal height.

(d) Calculate the range.

2 A school wanted to investigate how long Year 9 pupils spent on their homework each evening. A sample of 50 pupils were surveyed.

(a) Copy and complete this frequency table.

Number of hours	Frequency	Total time spent
$\frac{1}{2}$ hour	2	
1 hour	8	
$1\frac{1}{2}$ hours	17	
2 hours	19	
$2\frac{1}{2}$ hours	4	
Total		

(b) Calculate the mean, median and modal number of hours spent by this group of Year 9 pupils on their homework each evening.

3 A spelling test of ten words was given to 31 pupils every week for six consecutive weeks. Their total marks (out of 60) are given below.

19	27	18	30	28	13	20	25	25	37
41	50	46	8	54	47	19	27	29	37
27	18	41	14	35	10	32	11	31	32
15									

(a) Calculate the mean total spelling score of these 31 pupils.

(b) Find the range of their scores.

(c) Group the data, using three equal-sized class intervals.
Draw a frequency table to show how many scores there are in each group and then draw a frequency polygon to display the results.

(d) Group the data, this time using five equal-sized class intervals.
Draw a frequency table to show how many scores there are in each group.
Draw a frequency polygon using the same axes as in part (c) to demonstrate these results.

(e) Compare the two frequency polygons and comment on any differences.

Finding the mean from grouped data

When data is grouped, some information is lost but the data becomes easier to handle.

One hundred people were asked how far they had travelled to attend a concert. The distances were measured in kilometres. Then the data was grouped and recorded in this table.

> greater than
< less than
$\geqslant$ greater than or equal to
$\leqslant$ less than or equal to

Distance travelled (d km)	Frequency
$0 \leqslant d < 20$	25
$20 \leqslant d < 40$	38
$40 \leqslant d < 60$	23
$60 \leqslant d < 80$	10
$80 \leqslant d < 100$	4

$20 \leqslant d < 40$ means that the distance travelled is greater than or equal to 20 km but less than 40 km.

The *exact* distance travelled by each person was not recorded. Therefore, the exact mean cannot be calculated because, for that, the exact distance travelled by each individual is needed.

However, an **estimated mean** can be calculated by *approximating* the distance travelled by each individual.

The 25 people in the first group have each travelled a distance between 0 and 20 kilometres. It can be estimated that they have each travelled approximately 10 km, 10 being midway between 0 and 20.

The approximate distance travelled altogether by these 25 people is:

25 × 10 km = 250 km

The table can be extended to include this information.

Distance travelled (d km)	Frequency	Mid interval value (km)	Total distance (km)
$0 \leq d < 20$	25	10	$25 \times 10 = 250$
$20 \leq d < 40$	38	30	$38 \times 30 = 1140$
$40 \leq d < 60$	23	50	$23 \times 50 = 1150$
$60 \leq d < 80$	10	70	$10 \times 70 = 700$
$80 \leq d < 100$	4	90	$4 \times 90 = 360$
	Total 100		Total 3600

Key fact

An estimated mean is calculated from data in a grouped frequency table.

An **estimated mean** can then be calculated using the approximations in the table above.

$$\text{estimated mean distance travelled} = \frac{\text{estimated total distance travelled}}{\text{number of people travelling}}$$

$$= \frac{3600\,\text{km}}{100}$$

$$= 36\,\text{km}$$

Exercise 2

1 The time customers waited to be served at a supermarket checkout is recorded in the grouped frequency table below.

Waiting time (t minutes)	$0 \leq t < 2$	$2 \leq t < 4$	$4 \leq t < 6$	$6 \leq t < 8$	$8 \leq t < 10$
Frequency	15	31	9	4	1

(a) From this data, create a table including extra columns for the mid-interval values and the total waiting time for each group.

(b) Calculate the estimated mean waiting time at the checkout.

2 This table shows the amount of money raised by pupils on a sponsored walk.

Money raised (£ r)	$0 \leq r < 10$	$10 \leq r < 20$	$20 \leq r < 30$	$30 \leq r < 40$	$40 \leq r < 50$
Frequency	18	30	23	17	12

From this data, create a table including the extra columns you will need to calculate the estimated mean amount of sponsor money raised.

3 (a) Copy the grouped frequency table from Question 3 in Exercise 1 when the data was grouped in five class intervals.

(b) Calculate the estimated mean.

(c) Compare this with the actual mean calculated from the raw data. How accurate is your estimate?

Assignment 1 How heavy are your school bags?

Remember to have between 5 and 8 groups for the data.

You will need a set of bathroom scales or a spring balance.

- Find the weight of everyone's school bag in your class.
- Collect the data on the board and then decide how to group it using a frequency table.
- Calculate the estimated mean weight for your class's school bags.
- Draw a frequency polygon to display the data.
- Collect the same data from at least 30 pupils in a different year group.
- Calculate the estimated mean and draw a frequency polygon on the same axes that you used for your own class.
- Compare the results for the two classes.
- What do the results tell you? Can you draw any conclusions?
- What factors might have affected the results?

Considering the spread

A distribution is described as **uniform** if the frequency of each group is the same.

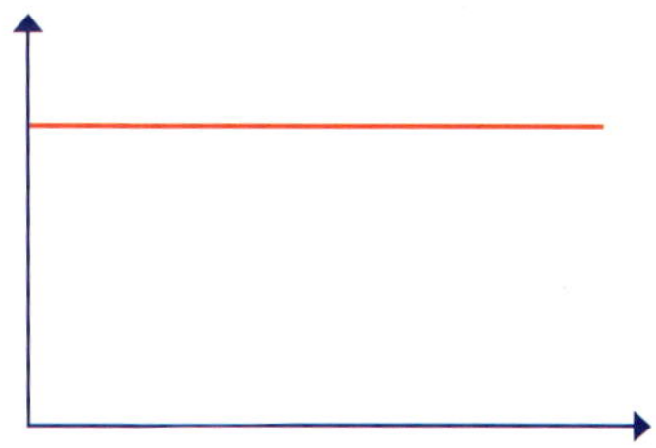

A uniform distribution

Second class letters tend to be delivered on the second day after posting.

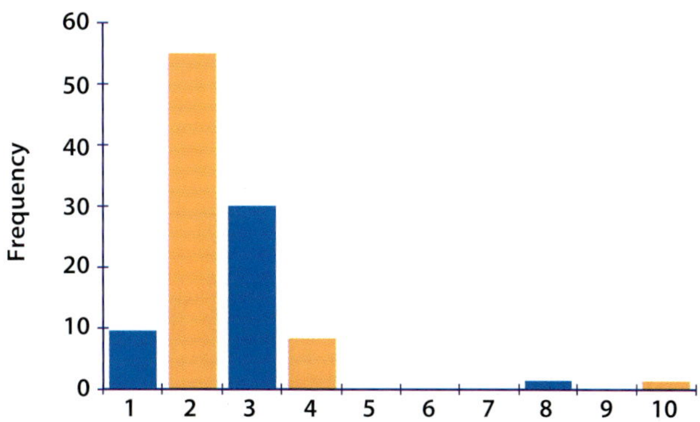

Number of days taken to deliver second class letters

The distribution of the data is not uniform and the mean is less typical of the sample.

Using the mean as a measure of the average of this type of distribution is therefore not appropriate.

Exercise 3

1 Ten friends completed a marathon race. Their times to complete the race are shown below.

2 hrs 45 mins	**2 hrs 52 mins**	**2 hrs 54 mins**
2 hrs 59 mins	**3 hrs 2 mins**	**3 hrs 10 mins**
3 hrs 12 mins	**3 hrs 12 mins**	
3 hrs 23 mins	**5 hrs 15 mins**	

(a) Calculate the mean time taken to complete the marathon race.

(b) Calculate the range of times taken.

(c) Calculate the percentage of runners taking more than the mean time to complete their marathon.

(d) Explain whether the mean is a good measure of the average time taken.

2 Forty households were surveyed, and the number of children in each family was recorded:

Number of children in family	0	1	2	3	4	5
Frequency	6	12	17	2	2	1

(a) Calculate the mean number of children per family.

(b) Write down the range for this data.

(c) Draw a bar chart to show these results and comment on the shape of the chart.

(d) Calculate the percentage of families with more than the mean number of children in their family.

Cumulative frequency

Key fact

The cumulative frequency is the total number of data items up to a particular value.

The median of a set of data items is the middle value if all values are written in an order. Therefore 50% of the items are above the median and 50% below.

When data is grouped, the actual values of particular items are not recorded. Finding an estimate for the median now involves drawing a **cumulative frequency graph.**

Here is the data from Exercise 2, Question 1, for which cumulative values have been calculated.

Waiting time (t secs)	Frequency	Waiting time (t secs)	Cumulative frequency	Points to plot
$0 \leq t < 2$	15	< 2	15	(2, 15)
$2 \leq t < 4$	31	< 4	46	(4, 46)
$4 \leq t < 6$	9	< 6	55	(6, 55)
$6 \leq t < 8$	4	< 8	59	(8, 59)
$8 \leq t < 10$	1	< 10	60	(10, 60)

For the cumulative frequency graph, the cumulative frequencies are plotted against the upper boundaries of the class intervals.

No customer had to wait less than 0 minutes, so the cumulative frequency graph begins at (0,0).

The table then shows that, for example, 46 customers had to wait *less than four* minutes, so a point is plotted at (4, 46). A total of 55 customers waited less than six minutes, so another point is plotted at (6, 55).

Notice that the points are joined with a smooth curve, *not* with straight lines.

The graph also shows how the estimated median can then be found.

- Finding a half of the total number of people sampled

  $\frac{1}{2}$ of 60 = 30

- Reading from the cumulative frequency graph the time which corresponds to a cumulative frequency of 30

This can be seen, from the graph, to be approximately three minutes.

Exercise 4

1 (a) Complete a cumulative frequency table for the data in Question 2 of Exercise 2 on page 38.

(b) Draw a cumulative frequency graph and estimate the median.

2 The weights of 95 pupils were recorded and are shown in this frequency table.

Weight (w kg)	$40 \leqslant w < 45$	$45 \leqslant w < 50$	$50 \leqslant w < 55$	$55 \leqslant w < 60$	$60 \leqslant w < 65$	$65 \leqslant w < 70$	$70 \leqslant w < 75$
Frequency	3	2	4	17	44	20	5

None of the pupils recorded had a weight less than 40 kg.

(a) Create a cumulative frequency table and draw the cumulative frequency graph.

(b) From your cumulative frequency graph, estimate the median weight of these 95 pupils.

3 (a) Copy and complete this cumulative frequency table.

Time spent listening to music (t hours per week)	Frequency	Time spent	Cumulative frequency
$5 \leqslant t < 10$	5		
$10 \leqslant t < 15$	12		
$15 \leqslant t < 20$	21		
$20 \leqslant t < 25$	25		
$25 \leqslant t < 30$	18		
$30 \leqslant t < 35$	9		

(b) Draw the cumulative frequency graph and estimate the median for this data.

4 (a) Using the data collected in Assignment 1 (page 39), compare the estimated medians for the weight of school bags from the two year groups.

(b) Comment on the medians. Explain which of the median or the mean is the more appropriate measure of this average.

Quartiles

Key fact

25% of data items are less than the lower quartile.

75% of data items are less than the upper quartile.

The median divides the data into halves.

In a similar way, quartiles divide data into quarters.

The **lower quartile** is the median of the data *below* the median.

The **upper quartile** is the median of the data *above* the median.

The **interquartile range** is the difference between the upper and lower quartile and is important because it shows the spread of the middle half of the data.

Example

Find the median, lower quartile, upper quartile and interquartile range of these heights (in centimetres).

162 156 169 160 163 173 169

First, put the items into ascending order of size.

156	160	162	163	169	169	173
	↑ Lower quartile		Median		↑ Upper quartile	

The interquartile range is the difference between the upper and lower quartiles.

169 cm − 160 cm = 9 cm

When the data has been grouped, the quartiles and interquartile range can be read from the cumulative frequency graph.

Exercise 5

1 The time taken (in minutes) to draw a cumulative frequency graph was recorded for 12 pupils.

6 10 5 4 9 7 6 9 11 8 5 4

(a) Find the median.

(b) Find the upper and lower quartiles.

(c) Calculate the interquartile range.

2 Using the cumulative frequency graph drawn in Question 2 in Exercise 4, estimate:

(a) the lower quartile

(b) the upper quartile

(c) the interquartile range.

3 Using the cumulative frequency graph drawn in Question 3 in Exercise 4, estimate:

(a) the lower quartile

(b) the upper quartile

(c) the interquartile range.

4 Using the cumulative frequency graph drawn in Question 4 in Exercise 4, estimate:

(a) the lower quartile

(b) the upper quartile

(c) the interquartile range.

5 Here are the marks gained by 80 pupils in a Mathematics test, out of 100.

Marks (m)	$0 \leqslant m < 20$	$20 \leqslant m < 40$	$40 \leqslant m < 60$	$60 \leqslant m < 80$	$80 \leqslant m < 100$
Frequency	2	12	29	31	6

(a) By drawing a cumulative frequency graph, find

(i) the median,

(ii) the lower and upper quartiles and

(iii) the interquartile range.

(b) If the pass mark was 50, estimate what percentage of pupils passed the exam.

(c) If eight pupils were awarded a certificate of commendation, estimate the lowest mark needed to obtain a certificate.

(d) Calculate the 80th percentile.

Key fact

Percentiles divide a cumulative frequency distribution into 100 parts.

Box plots

Box plots are sometimes called box-and-whisker diagrams.

A box plot displays the quartiles of a set of data items.

Example

Here are the statistics for the height data from the example on page 42.

Lower quartile: 160 cm

Median: 163 cm

Upper quartile: 169 cm

Interquartile range: 169 cm – 160 cm = 9 cm

Range: 173 cm – 156 cm = 17 cm

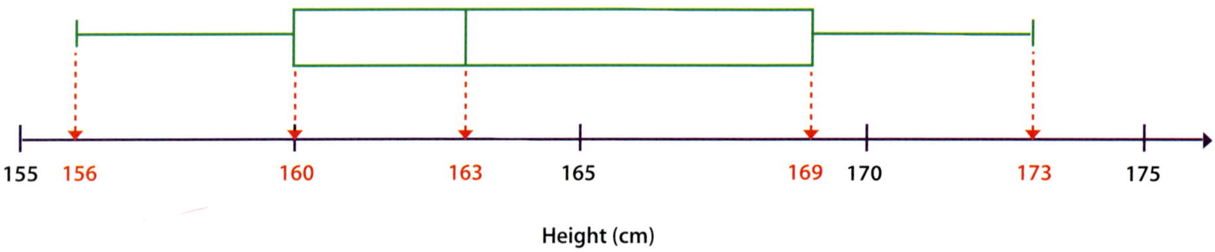

Assignment 2 Understanding the box plot

- Which part of the data is included in the box?
- How is the median shown?
- What do the 'whiskers' show?
- Which parts of the diagram show the lower and upper quartiles?
- How does this type of display help you to explain the spread of the data?

Exercise 6

1 During a local angling competition, 30 fish were caught and weighed.

(a) Display this information using a box plot.

Weight of fish (kg)				
Smallest	Lower quartile	Median	Upper quartile	Highest
2.0	3.9	4.2	4.5	5.2

(b) What do you notice from the box plot?

2 Two assistants serve chips in the school canteen. Fifty pupils were each served by both assistants and the results analysed as shown below.

Number of chips served per portion					
	Lowest	Lower quartile	Median	Upper quartile	Greatest
Assistant A	15	16	17	19	24
Assistant B	16	18	18.5	19	21

(a) Draw box plots to display this information.

(b) Which assistant would you choose to serve your chips? Explain why.

3 Two different Mathematics examinations were given to one group of Year 9 pupils. The marks were given as a percentage in each case and the results analysed as shown below.

Marks obtained in examinations as a percentage					
	Lowest	Lower quartile	Median	Upper quartile	Highest
Exam 1	42	65	80	85	92
Exam 2	34	48	62	78	94

(a) Draw box plots to display this information.

(b) Compare the results of the two examinations. What conclusions can you draw?

4 A box and whisker diagram can be used to compare the length of words used in a tabloid newspaper with those used in a broadsheet newspaper.

Make a tally chart to record the number of letters used in each word in a sample of 100 words from each kind of newspaper.

From your results for each paper find:

(a) the number of letters in the shortest word

(b) the number of letters in the longest word

(c) the median of the letters

(d) the lower and upper quartiles.

Use the information you have collected to draw a box plot for each newspaper and compare the results. Write down what you notice.

Assignment 3 Comparing pulse rates

- Measure the pulse rate of at least 30 pupils before and after exercise, using a stop-watch to time how long it takes for 60 pulse beats.
- Use the statistical methods you have learnt in this chapter to compare the results.
- Choose the most appropriate method to display the data.
- Draw conclusions from the statistical evidence collected.

Introduction to trigonometry

In this chapter you will learn:

- → **the basic facts about tangents, sines and cosines**
- → **how to use trigonometry to solve right-angled triangle problems.**

Starting points

Before starting this chapter, you will need:

- to know how to use a scientific calculator
- a knowledge of ratio.

Tangents

Key fact

A tangent is a line that touches a circle. It is perpendicular to a radius.

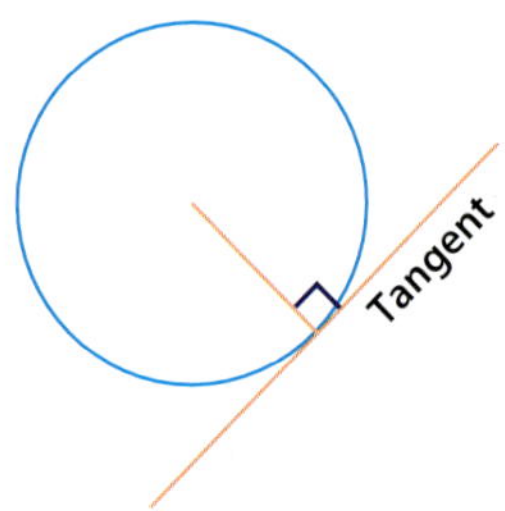

Assignment 1 **Lengths of tangent sections**

- Draw a circle with radius 1 unit in the bottom left-hand corner of your graph paper.

  (Use a scale of 2.5 cm to 1 unit.)

- Draw a tangent to the circle, perpendicular to the radius as shown.
- Draw in 'spokes' at 10° intervals and extend them to meet the tangent.
- Measure the length of the section of tangent cut off by each 'spoke'.

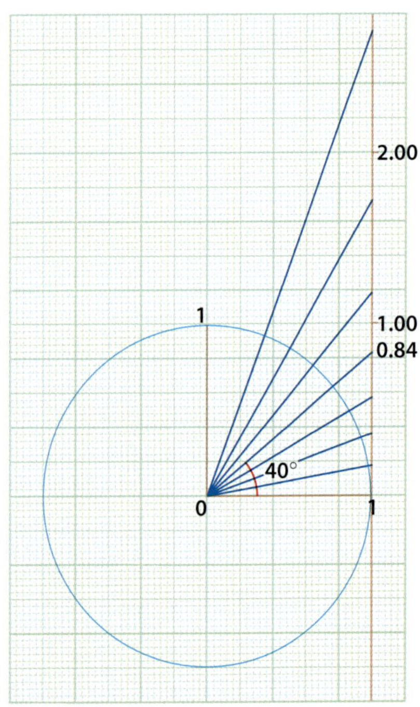

- Copy and complete this table of results.

Angle	Length of tangent section
0°	
10°	
20°	
30°	
40°	0.84
50°	
60°	
70°	

- Write down anything that you notice.
- What do you think is the length of the tangent section cut off by the spoke at 90°?

Triangles and tangents

The table obtained in Assignment 1 can be used to calculate the height of right-angled triangles which have a base length of 1 unit.

Example

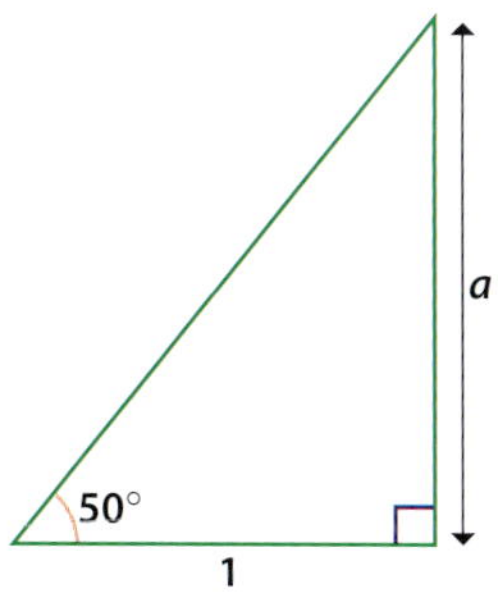

a = length of tangent for a spoke at 50°
= 1.2

Thus, in general terms:

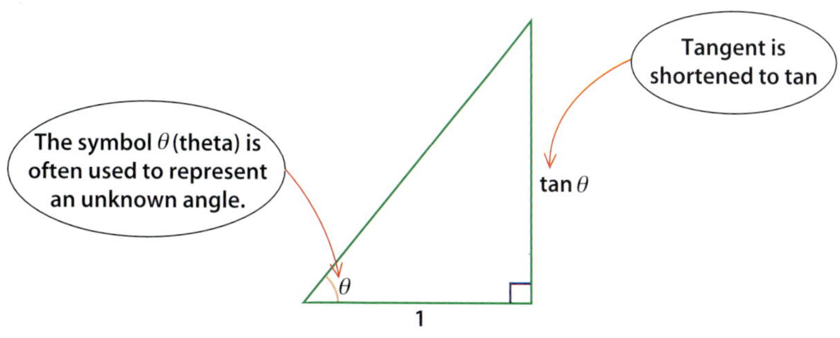

Exercise 1

1 Using the same method given in the Example (to find *a*), find the sides or angles marked with the letters *b* to *i* in these triangles.

Draw each triangle and show your working.

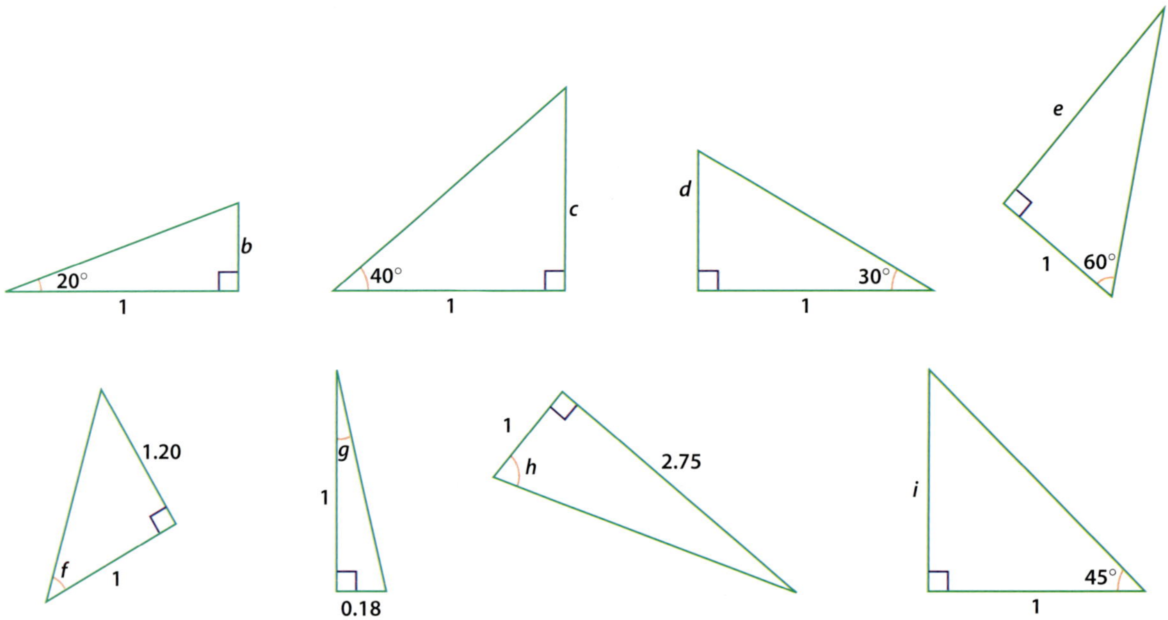

Using a calculator

The table obtained in Assignment 1 is for tens of degrees and is accurate to only two places of decimals.

There is usually a need to find the tangent of any angle to a greater degree of accuracy. For this, you can use a scientific calculator.

Example

To find: tan 52.7°

Either press [5] [2] [·] [7] then [tan] [=]

or press [tan] then [5] [2] [·] [7] [=]

> **You will need to find out which operating logic your calculator uses.**

You should obtain 1.312687636 on a 10-digit display calculator, or 1.3126876 on an 8-digit calculator.

Inverse tangents

Sometimes, you know the lengths of the sides of a triangle but want to find out the size of an angle. For this you can use the inverse tangent.

Example

To find: the angle of the spoke given that the length of the tangent section is 0.335

This is an *inverse* process and you will need to press the [inv] button

On some calculators you may need to press [2nd] or [shift]

Either press [0] [·] [3] [3] [5]

then [inv] [tan] [=]

or press [inv] [tan]

then [0] [·] [3] [3] [5] [=]

Your display should show 18.5° (to 1 d.p.).

Inverse tangent is shortened to $\tan^{-1}$.

Example

Use your calculator to check that

$\tan^{-1}(2.5) = 68.2°$ (to 1 d.p.)

Exercise 2

1 Find, correct to 3 significant figures, the tangents of these angles:

(a) 32° (b) 56° (c) 89°
(d) 12.7° (e) 78.2° (f) 4.3°
(g) 89.9° (h) 37.25° (i) 0.09°
(j) 49.47° (k) 45° (l) 63.44°

2 Find, correct to 1 decimal place, the angles for these tangents:

(a) 0.9 (b) 4.0 (c) 0.81
(d) 6.31 (e) 0.63 (f) 1.45
(g) 2.5 (h) 0.866 (i) 0.75
(j) 0.6 (k) 0.5 (l) $\sqrt{3}$

3 What is the value of $\tan 90°$?

Tangents and enlargement

You can use a calculator to find the length of the tangent section for any angle provided the base length of the triangle is 1 unit.

However, the length of the base is rarely 1 unit. When this is the case, you will need to use your knowledge of enlargements.

Example

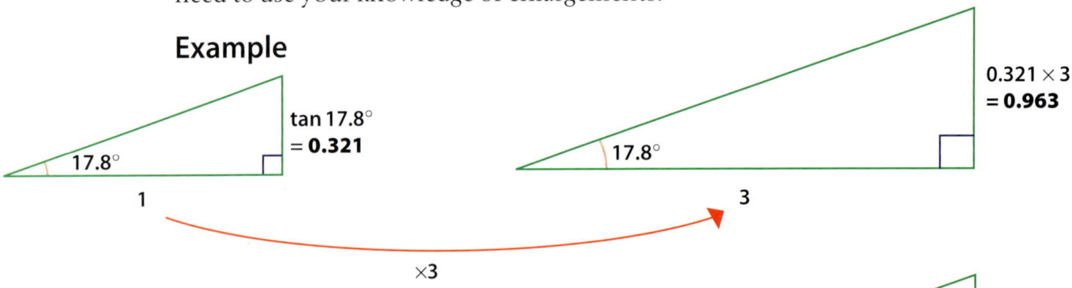

In general,

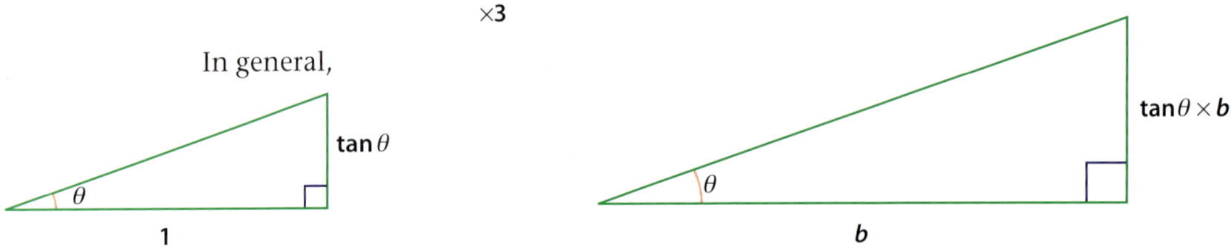

Exercise 3

1 Copy each of these triangles and calculate, correct to 3 significant figures, the length of the lettered sides *a* to *j*. (These triangles are *not* drawn to scale.)

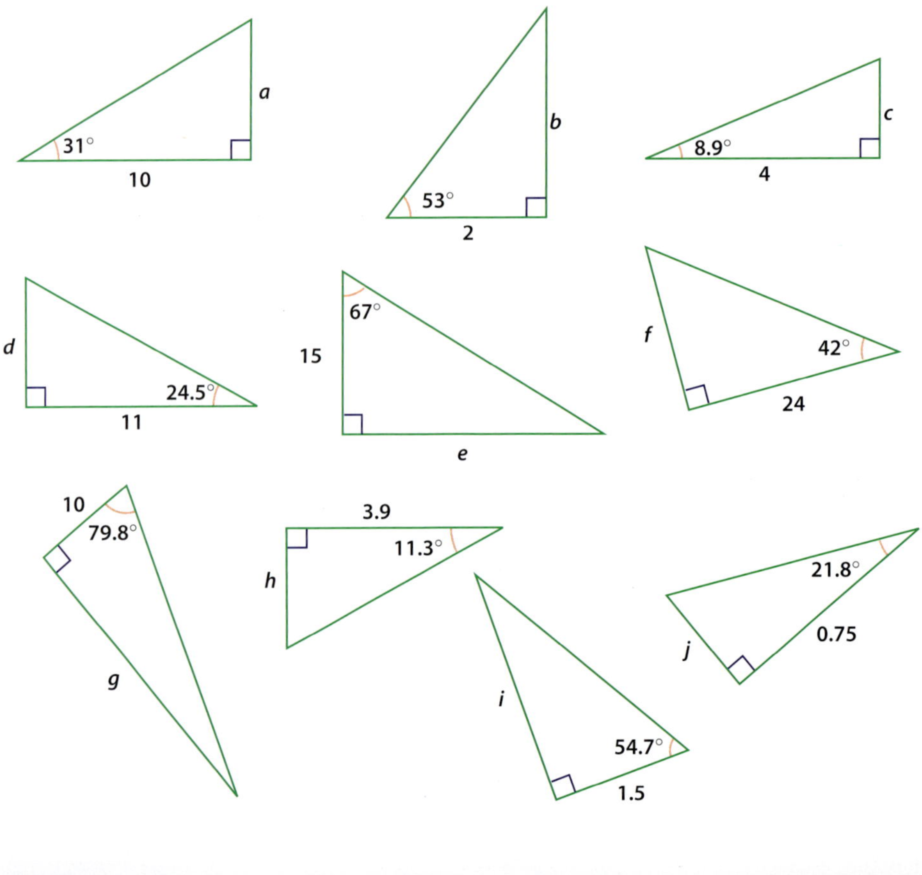

Finding angles

Example

Find the size of angle x.

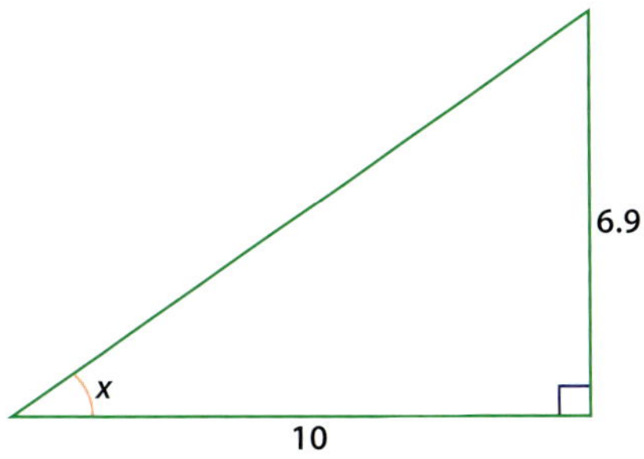

If you divide all the lengths of the triangle by 10 you obtain:

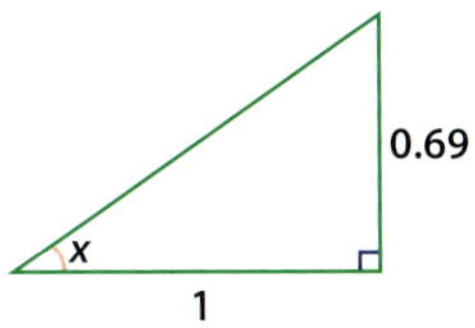

$$\tan x = 0.69$$
$$x = \tan^{-1}(0.69)$$
$$= 34.6°$$

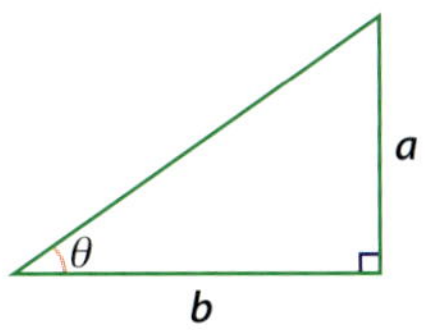

In general,

$$\tan\theta = \frac{a}{b}$$

Exercise 4

1 Copy these triangles and calculate the angles labelled a to h, correct to 1 d.p.

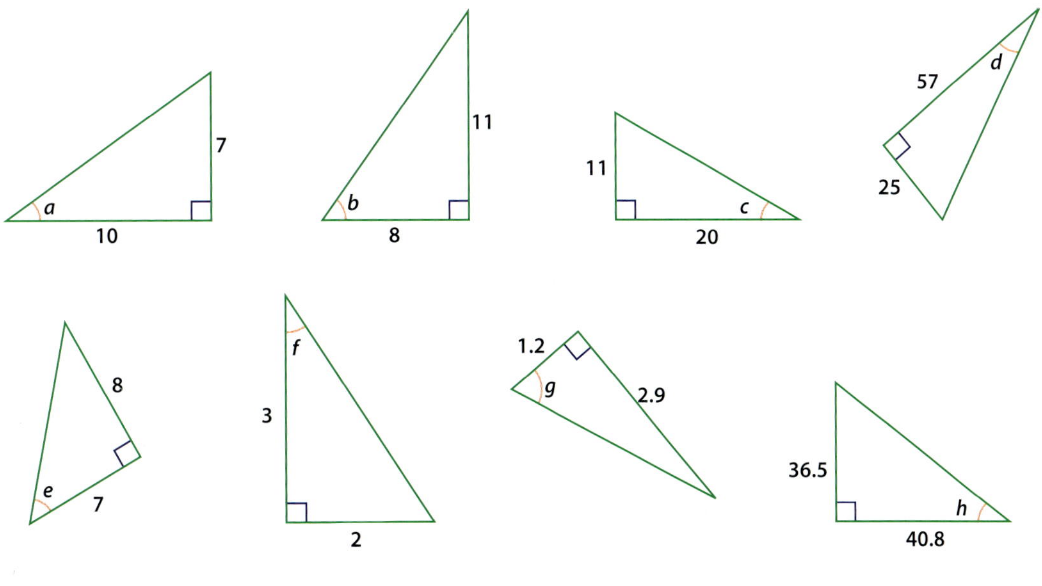

Assignment 2 The coordinates of points on a circle

- Draw a quarter-circle with radius 1 unit.
  Use a scale of 10 cm for each 1 unit.
- Draw in 'spokes' at 10° intervals.

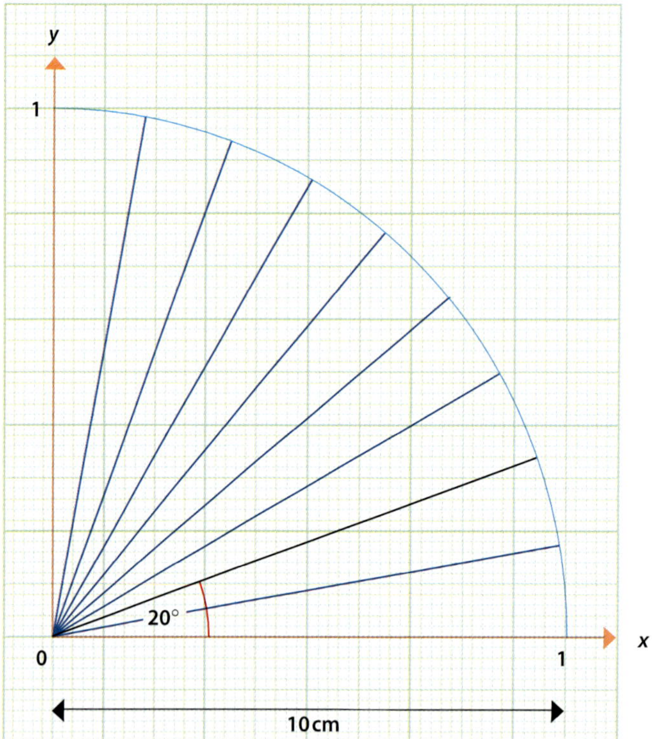

- Copy and complete this table for each angle (measured from the *x*-axis).

- Write in the corresponding *x* and *y* coordinates.
  (Two have been done for you already.)
- Write down anything that you notice.

Angle	x	y
0°		
10°		
20°	0.94	0.34
30°		
40°		
50°		
60°		
70°		
80°		
90°	0.00	1.00

Sines, cosines and triangles

In a right-angled triangle with a hypotenuse of length 1 unit, the x coordinate (which is adjacent to the angle) is the cosine of the angle.

The y coordinate (which is opposite the angle) is the sine of the angle.

Consider the values from the table on page 52:

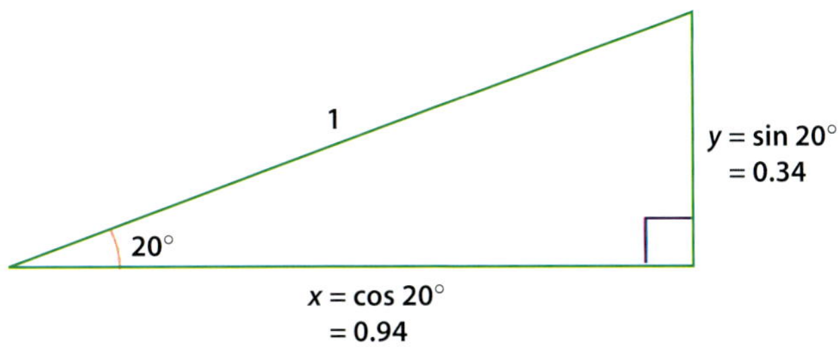

Sine is shortened to sin.

Cosine is shortened to cos.

Thus, in general terms, if the hypotenuse is 1 unit:

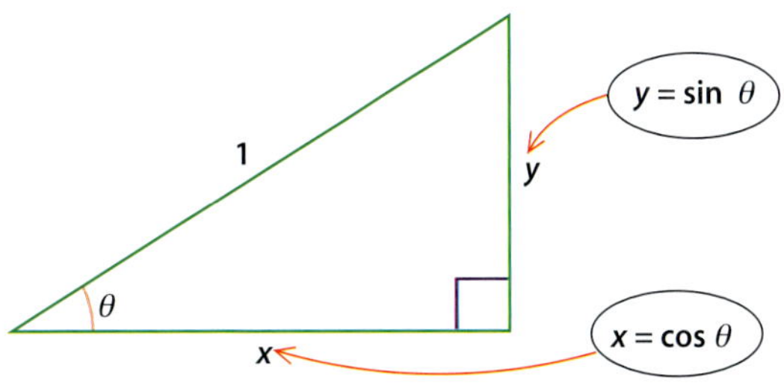

Exercise 5

1 Use your table from Assignment 2 to find the sides or angles marked with the letters a to k. Draw each triangle and show your working. Give your answers correct to 2 sig. figs.

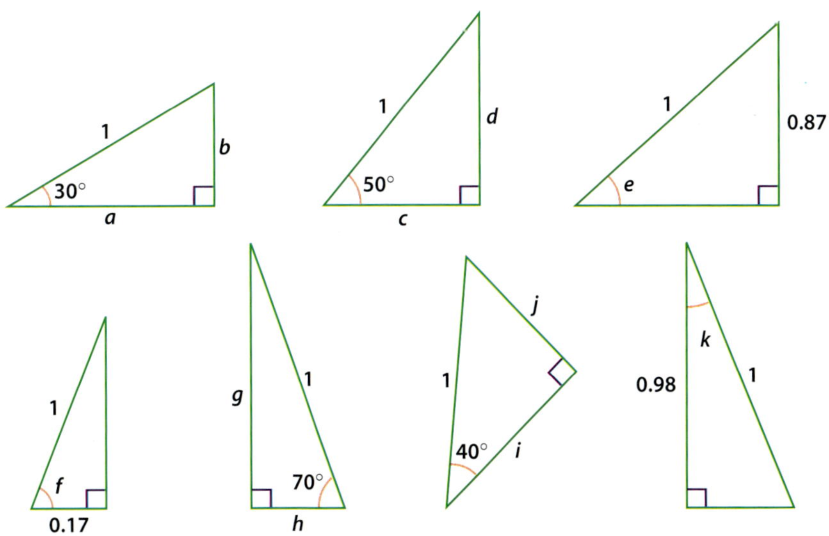

Sines and cosines and enlargements

The sine and cosine of any angle can be found using the **sin** or **cos** buttons on a scientific calculator.

The length of the hypotenuse is rarely 1 unit.

Again, you can use your knowledge of enlargements to overcome this problem.

If the hypotenuse is a multiple of 1 unit, then the required length must also be multiplied by the same number.

Example

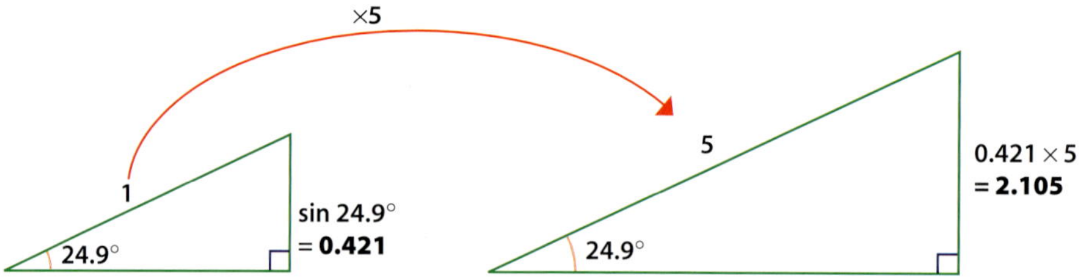

In general,

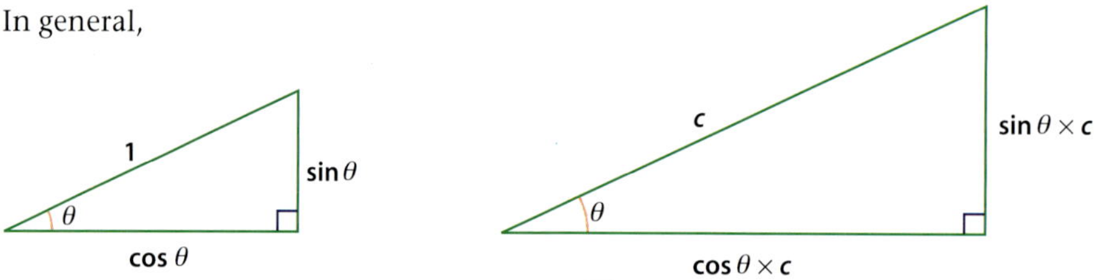

Exercise 6

1 Copy these triangles and calculate, correct to 3 significant figures, the lengths of the sides lettered a to j.

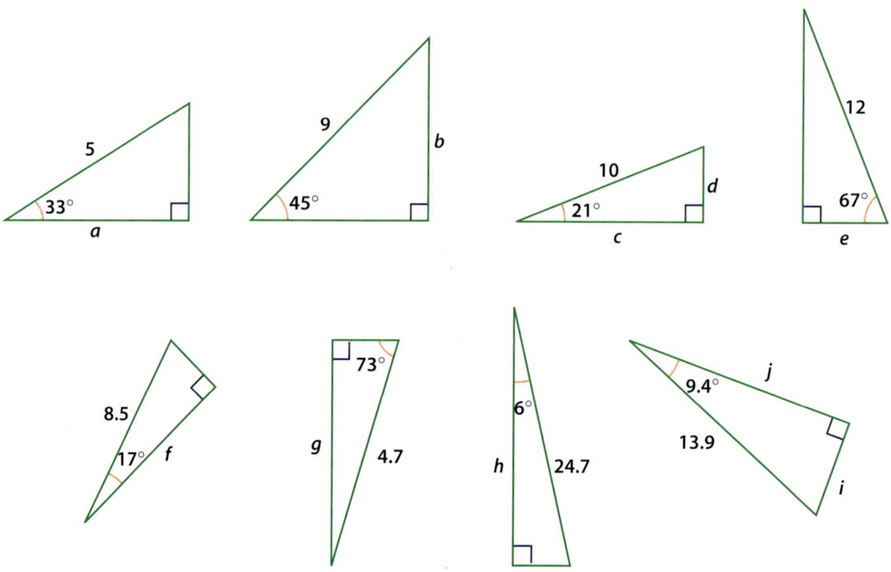

Finding angles

You can also find unknown angles in right-angled triangles using sines and cosines.

Example

To find: the size of angle θ

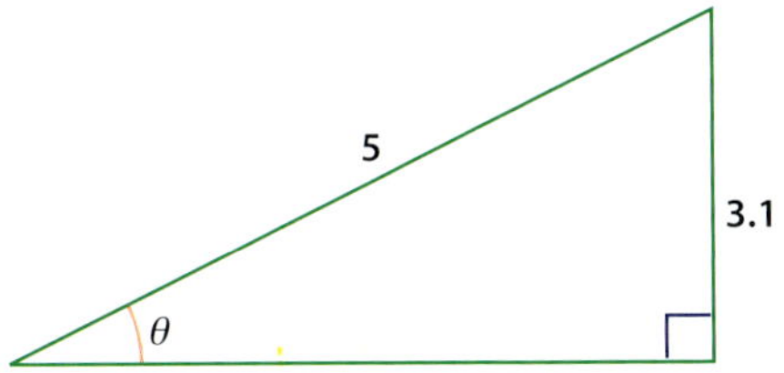

This is a sine problem.

If you divide all the lengths of the triangle by 5 you obtain:

Thus,

$\sin\theta = 0.62$

$\theta = \sin^{-1}(0.62)$

$= 38.3°$

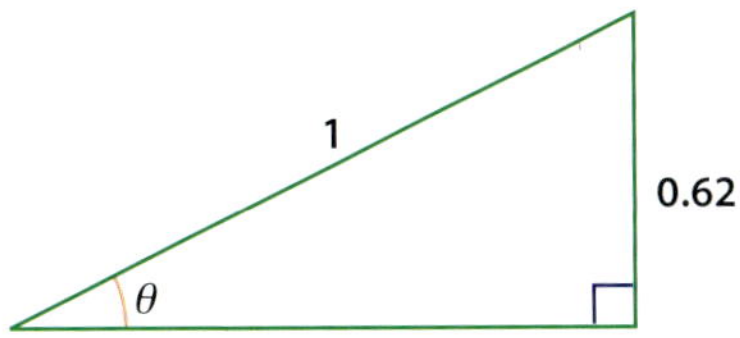

Sin^{-1} means inverse sine.

In general,

$\sin\theta = \frac{a}{c}$

$\cos\theta = \frac{b}{c}$

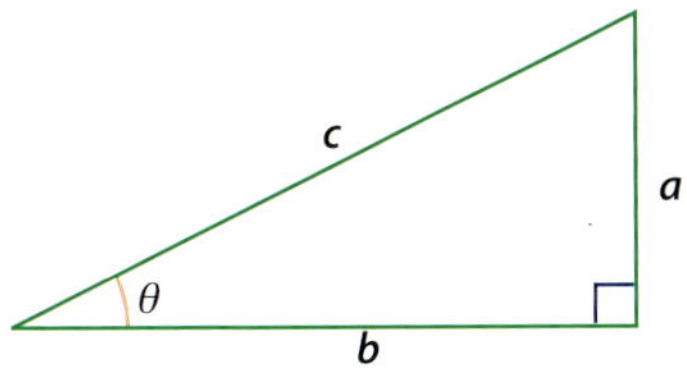

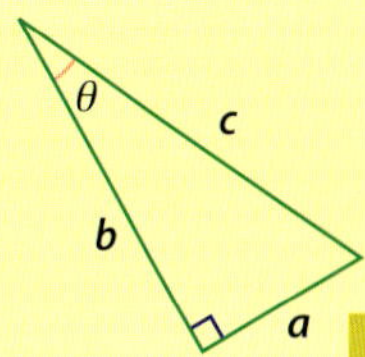

Exercise 7

1 Copy these triangles and calculate the angles lettered a to h correct to 1 d.p.

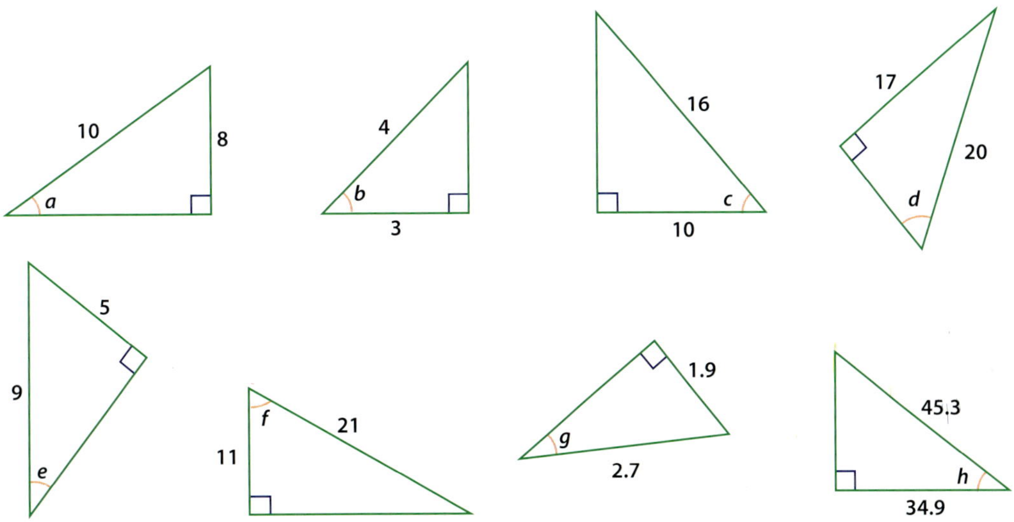

Naming the sides of a right-angled triangle

The longest side is called the **hypotenuse**.

The side opposite the angle θ is called the **opposite** side.

The side alongside the angle θ is called the **adjacent** side.

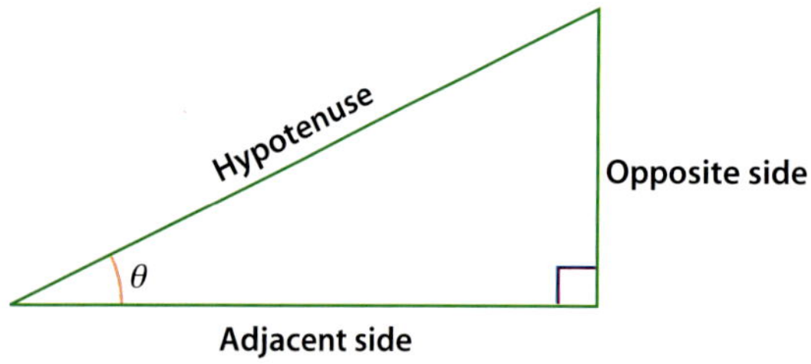

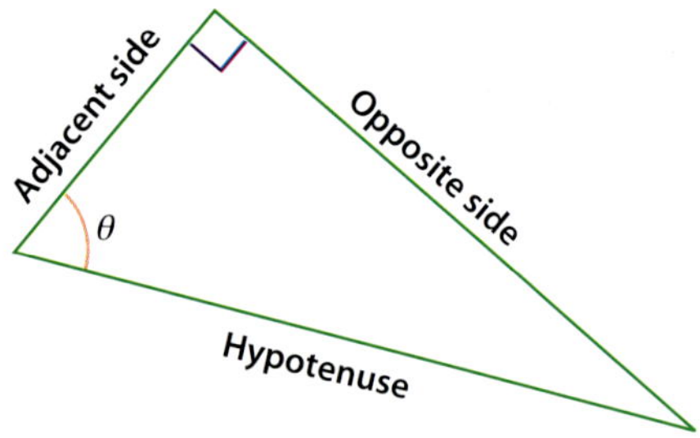

Exercise 8

1 For each of these triangles, identify which letters label the hypotenuse and the opposite and adjacent sides. The first one has been done for you.

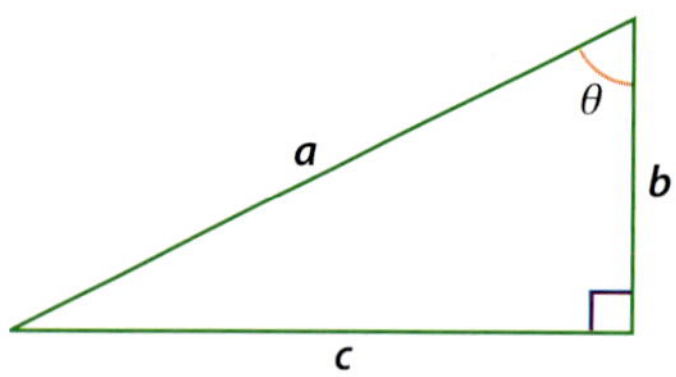

a is the hypotenuse.
b is the adjacent side.
c is the opposite side.

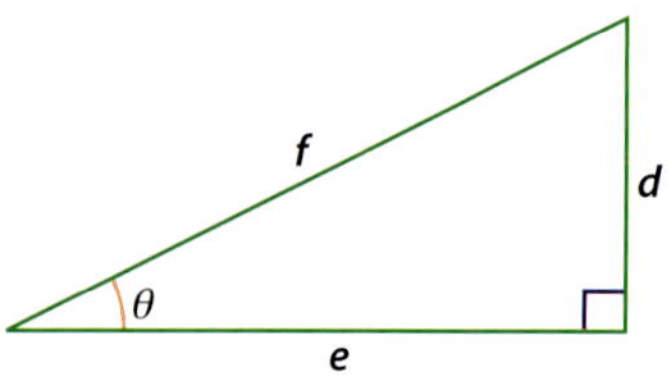

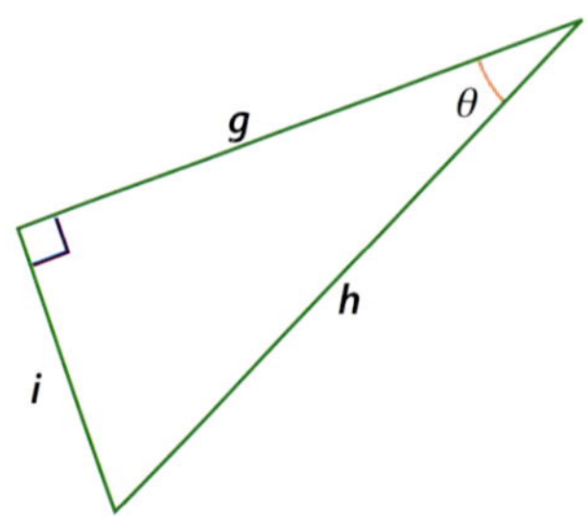

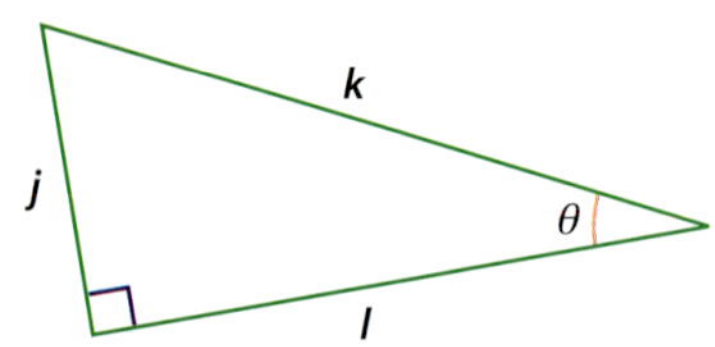

2 For this triangle, copy and complete these statements.

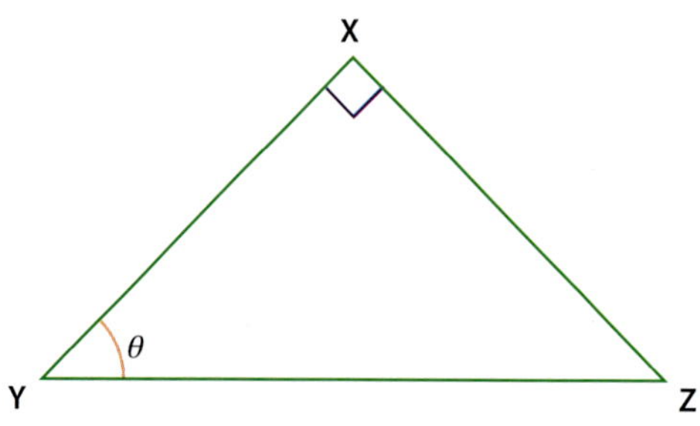

XY is the adjacent side.
XZ is the............
YZ is the............

Using sines, cosines and tangents

Collecting all the information from this topic:

For any right-angled triangle,

$a = \tan\theta \times b \Rightarrow \tan\theta = \frac{a}{b}$ or $\tan\theta = \frac{\text{opp}}{\text{adj}}$

$b = \cos\theta \times c \Rightarrow \cos\theta = \frac{b}{c}$ or $\cos\theta = \frac{\text{adj}}{\text{hyp}}$

$a = \sin\theta \times c \Rightarrow \sin\theta = \frac{a}{c}$ or $\sin\theta = \frac{\text{opp}}{\text{hyp}}$

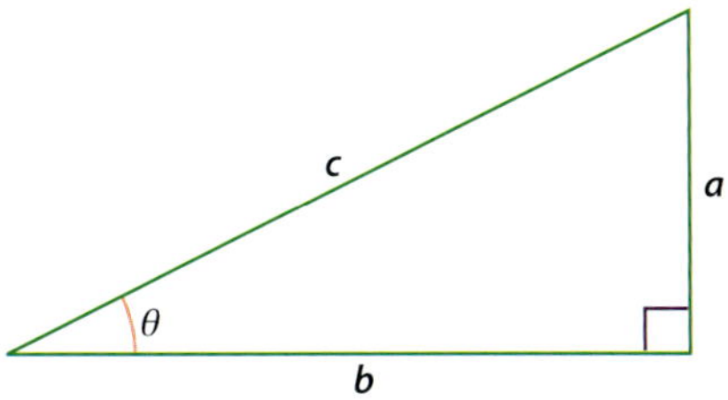

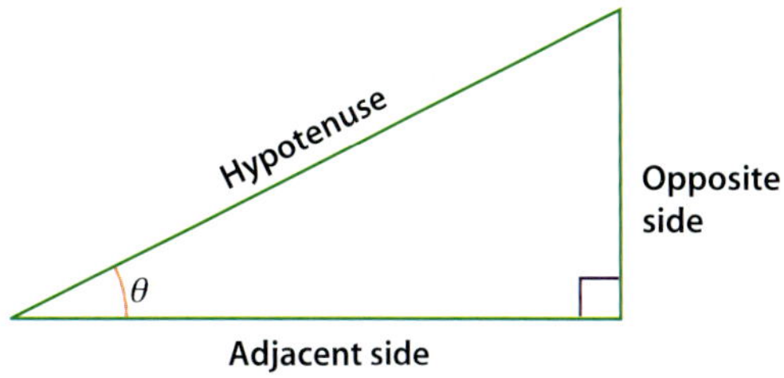

Key fact

$\sin\theta = \frac{\text{opp}}{\text{hyp}}$

$\cos\theta = \frac{\text{adj}}{\text{hyp}}$

$\tan\theta = \frac{\text{opp}}{\text{adj}}$

Check that you know where these formulæ come from.

It is important to learn these ratios.

It is also important to decide which formula to use and to show all working.

Example

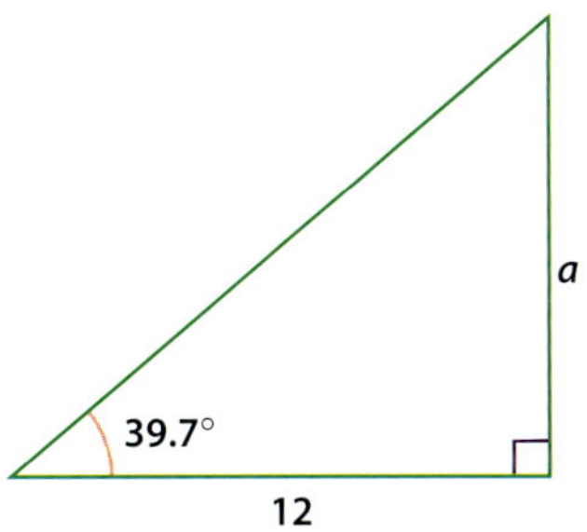

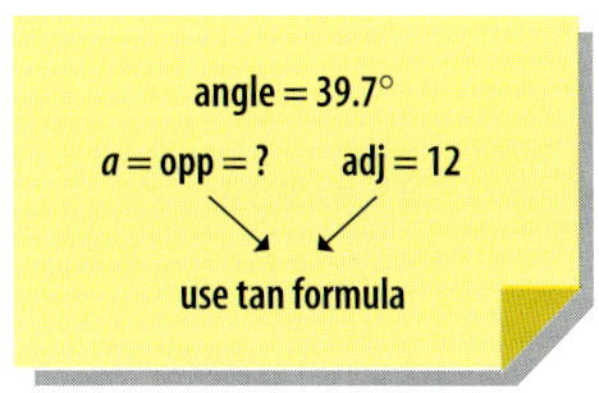

$a = \tan 39.7° \times 12$

$= 0.8302 \times 12$

$\simeq 9.96$ (to 3 sig.figs)

Exercise 9

1 For each of these triangles:

(a) choose the appropriate formula to calculate the lettered side or angle in each of these triangles

(b) copy the triangles and show all your working, giving your answers correct to 3 significant figures.

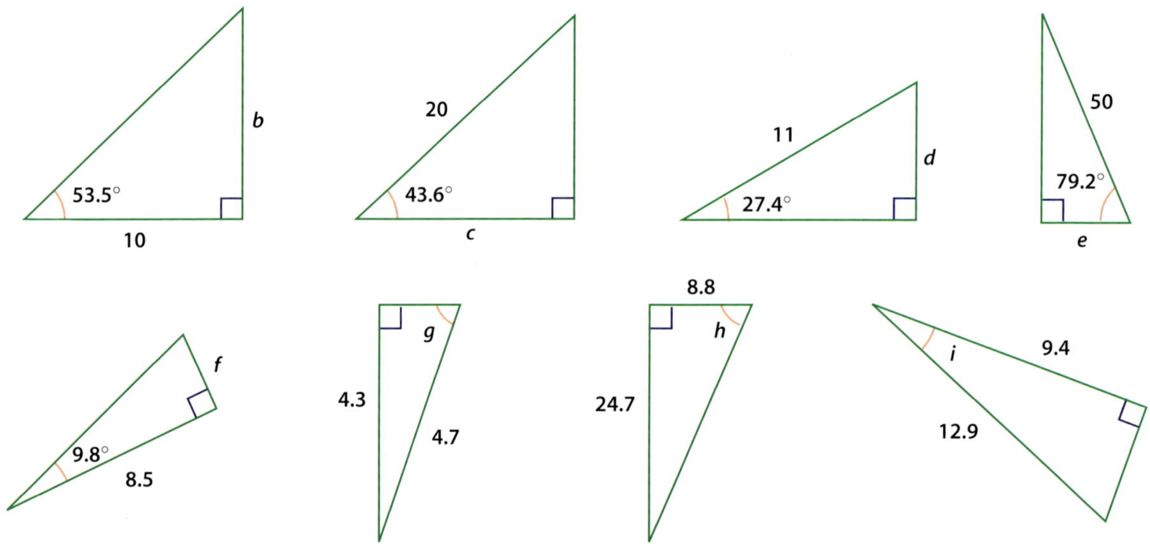

Practical uses of trigonometry

So far, all questions involving sines, cosines and tangents have been connected directly to right-angled triangles. This section considers practical problems where trigonometry can be a useful aid. In all problems, remember:

- to draw a diagram from the information provided if one is not given
- to establish whether the problem involves a sine, cosine or tangent
- to lay out your solution, step by step.

'Elevation' is the angle looking upwards from the horizontal.

Example

The angle of elevation of the top of a chimney at a distance of 150 metres is 20°. Find the height of the chimney.

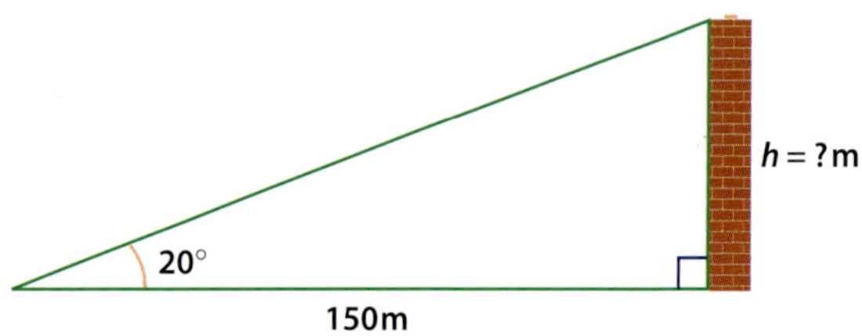

angle = 20°
h = opp = ? adj = 150
use tan formula

Let the height of the chimney be h metres. Then,

$h = \tan 20° \times 150$

$= 0.3640 \times 150$

$\simeq 54.6$ (to 3 sig.figs)

So, the height of the chimney is 54.6 metres.

Exercise 10

1 The angle of elevation of the top of a chimney at a distance of 65 metres is 35°. Calculate the height of the chimney.

2 A ladder, 8.5 metres long, just reaches the top of a vertical wall.

If the ladder makes an angle of 70° with the ground, calculate the height of the wall.

Calculate also, the distance of the foot of the ladder from the wall.

3 A ship sailed for 45 kilometres on a bearing of 034°.

How far north was the ship from its starting point?

4 The centre pole of a wigwam is 2.4 metres high.

The slanted sides which touch the ground are 3.1 metres long.

Calculate the angle between a slanted side and the ground.

5 The diagonal of a rectangle makes an angle of 30° with the longer sides of the shape.

(a) If each of the longer sides of the rectangle is 8 cm, what is the length of each of the shorter sides?

(b) Calculate the length of the diagonal.

6 The string of a kite is 200 m long and it makes an angle of 48° with the horizontal.

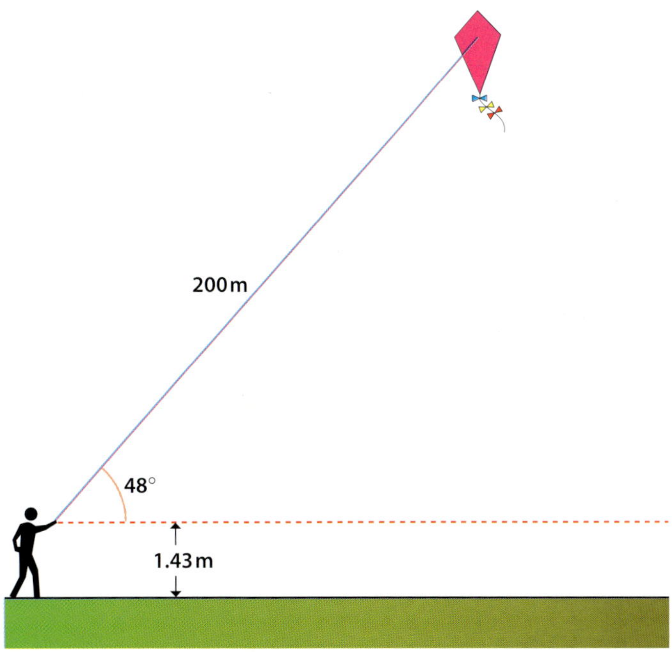

If the end of the string is held 1.43m above the ground, how high is the kite flying?

7 ΔABC is an equilateral triangle with sides of length 10 cm.

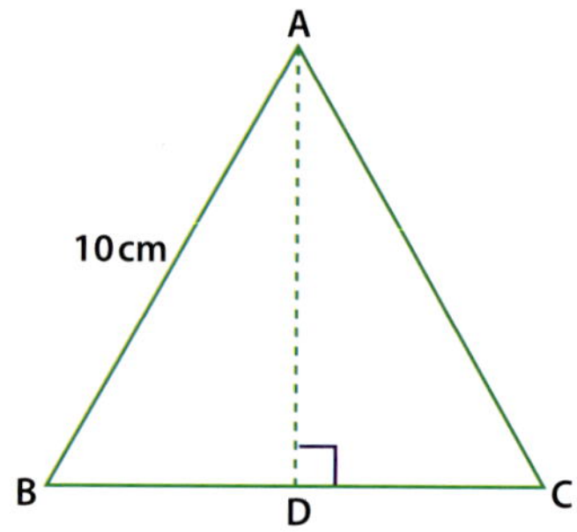

(a) Calculate the perpendicular height AD.

(b) Hence, find the area of the triangle, ABC.

8 PQRS is a field in the shape of a trapezium.

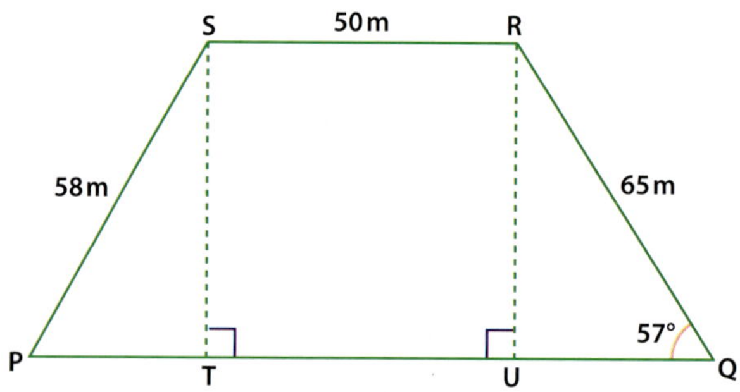

Calculate,

(a) the length QU

(b) the length RU

(c) the length PT

(d) the area of the field.

Solving simultaneous equations

In this chapter you will learn:

- → **how to solve simultaneous equations using graphs**
- → **how to solve simultaneous equations by substitution**
- → **how to solve simultaneous equations using the elimination method.**

Starting points

Before starting this chapter, you will need to be able to:

- plot straight line graphs
- change the subject of an equation
- substitute values into an expression
- recognise common factors.

Solving problems

Exercise 1

1 (a) Make a list of 12 possible solutions to this statement:

A book and a magazine cost £10.

(b) Explain why it is impossible to be sure about the cost of each item.

(c) The same book and two copies of the magazine cost £13. Use this additional information to find the cost of the book and the magazine.

2 A can of drink and a sandwich cost £1.10. If the cost of a drink is d pence, and the cost of a sandwich is s pence, this information can be written as

$d + s = 110$

(a) Write down ten possible solutions for d and s.

(b) Another can of the same drink and two of the same types of sandwich cost £1.70. Write this second statement algebraically and list ten possible solutions.

(c) Use the information from the two equations to find the cost of a can of drink.

3 For each of these pairs of equations, find the value of a and b which make each pair of equations correct.

(a) $a + b = 11$
$a + 2b = 13$

(b) $a + b = 5$
$a - b = 3$

(c) $2a + 2b = 16$
$3a + 2b = 21$

(d) $a + b = 6$
$a - b = 10$

(e) $a + b = 3\frac{1}{2}$
$2a + b = 5$

Try to work systematically.

4 Two families visit a theme park. In the first family, there are three adults and two children The cost for this family is £37.70. In the second family, there are two adults and four children. The cost for this family is £40.60.

(a) Write down an equation which represents the cost of each family's tickets.

(b) What is the cost of a ticket for an adult?

(c) What is the cost for a child?

Solving simultaneous equations using graphs

Key fact

To solve equations with two unknown values you need two equations.

To solve simultaneous equations you need to find values that fit both equations at the same time.

Pairs of values that satisfy one equation can be plotted as coordinates and joined to form a straight line. Pairs of values that satisfy another equation can also be plotted as coordinates and joined to form a second straight line on the same graph.

The solution of the two equations lies at the intersection of the two graphs, i.e. the point where the two lines cross. At this point, they have the same values.

Example

In Exercise 1, you found 12 pairs of values for the costs of a book and a magazine which added up to £10 and the same book and two magazines which cost £13.

These might have been

Book	+	Magazine	=	£10
£1	+	£9		
£2	+	£8		
£3	+	£7		
£4	+	£6		

Book	+	2 Magazines	=	£13
£1	+	2 × £6		
£2	+	2 × £5.50		
£3	+	2 × £5		
£4	+	2 × £4.50		

These two sets of values can be plotted as two straight lines on the same pair of axes.

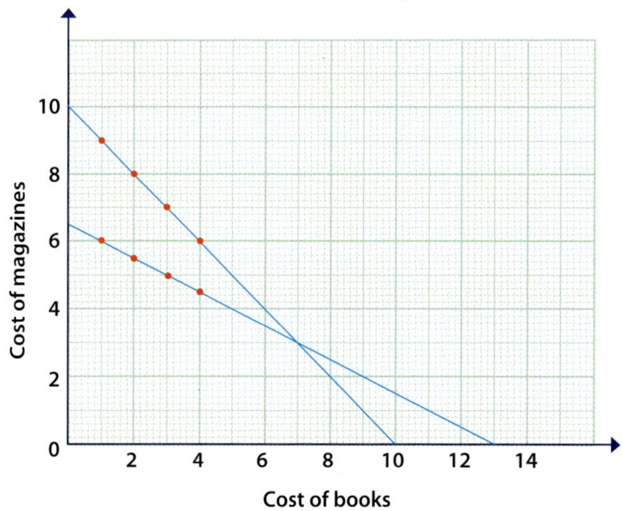

In this case, the intersection point of the two lines has coordinates (7, 3).
The solution to the problem is that the book costs £7 and the magazine costs £3.

The equations are labelled ① and ② to explain the working clearly.

The first step is to rewrite both equations in the form $y = mx + c$

Example

The sum of two numbers is 3, and their difference is –1.

This statement can be written algebraically as two simultaneous equations. Suppose the two numbers are x and y. Then

$x + y = 3$ ①

$x - y = -1$ ②

These two simultaneous equations can be solved to find the values of x and y.

Values that make both equations true can be calculated or the equations can be written in the form $y = mx + c$ and these can be plotted on a graph.

Equation ① can be rearranged by subtracting x from both sides:

$$x + y = 3$$
$$x - x + y = 3 - x$$
$$y = 3 - x$$

Equation ② can be rearranged by adding $y + 1$ to both sides:

$$x - y = -1$$
$$x - y + y + 1 = -1 + y + 1$$
$$x + 1 = y$$
$$y = x + 1$$

These two lines can be plotted on a graph.

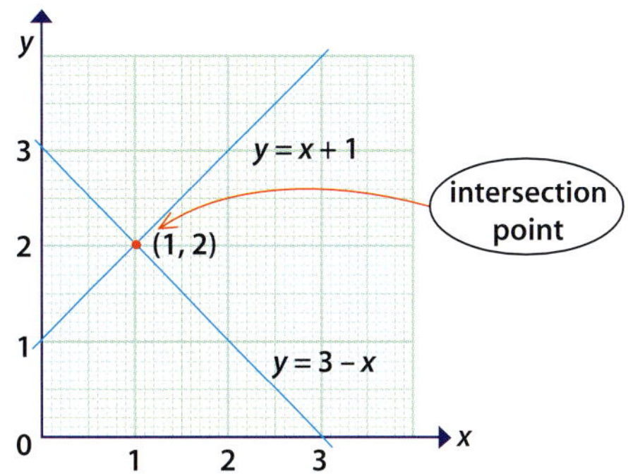

The values of x and y satisfying both equations are $x = 1$ and $y = 2$.

Exercise 2

1 (a) On a pair of axes, plot the graphs of these two equations: $x + y = 5$ and $x - y = 2$.

(b) Write down the coordinates of the point where the two lines cross.

(c) What values of x and y satisfy both equations?

2 Here are two simultaneous equations.

$x + y = 12$ ①

$2x + y = 19$ ②

(a) Find four pairs of values of x and y which make Equation ① correct.

(b) Find four pairs of values of x and y which make Equation ② correct.

(c) Plot your eight pairs of values of x and y on a single set of axes and join them to form two straight lines.

(d) Use your graph to find a solution which satisfies both equations.

3 For each of these pairs of simultaneous equations, plot the graphs of both equations on one set of axes.

In each case, use your graph to find the solutions to x and y which satisfy both equations.

Use the equation labels ① and ② to explain your working.

(a) $y = 3x - 1$ ①
$y = x + 3$ ②

(b) $y = 2x - 1$ ①
$y = \frac{1}{2}x + 2$ ②

(c) $y = x + \frac{1}{2}$ ①
$y = 2x - 1$ ②

(d) $y = x + 1$ ①
$y = 6 - x$ ②

4 For each of these pairs of simultaneous equations, rearrange both equations in the form $y = mx + c$.

Plot each pair of simultaneous equations on a new set of axes and use the graphs to find the solutions.

(a) $x - y = -3$ ①
$2x - y = -1$ ②

(b) $y - \frac{1}{2}x = 4$ ①
$y - x = 2$ ②

(c) $x - y = -1$ ①
$x + y = 8$ ②

(d) $3x - y = 2$ ①
$x - y = -2$ ②

Solving simultaneous equations by substitution

The rearranging and graphing of pairs of equations is not always the easiest nor the quickest way to solve a pair of simultaneous equations.

Simultaneous equations can always be solved algebraically.

Substitution is one of the algebraic methods.

Example

In a game of tennis, two people serve 11 aces between them. The difference between the number of aces they serve is 3. How many aces did they each serve?

This information could be written as a pair of equations.

Suppose the two people serve a and b aces.

$a + b = 11$ ①

$a - b = 3$ ②

Equation ② can be rewritten as

$a = b + 3$ ③

This value of a can now be substituted into Equation ①.

$$a + b = 11$$
$$(b + 3) + b = 11$$
$$2b + 3 = 11$$
$$2b = 8$$
$$b = 4$$

Replacing this value for b in Equation (1) gives

$a + 4 = 11$

therefore

$a = 7$

Now, to check these two values are correct, substitute

$a = 7$ and $b = 4$ into Equation (2).

$a - b = 3$

$7 - 4 = 3$ ✓

Exercise 3

1 Solve these pairs of simultaneous equations by substituting the value of one variable into the other equation.

Check your results by substituting your solutions into the other equation.

(a) $2a + b = 5$ (1)
$a + 3b = 5$ (2)

(b) $2x + 3y = 14$ (1)
$x + 2y = 8$ (2)

(c) $c + 2d = 5$ (1)
$c + d = 4$ (2)

(d) $2e + f = 16$ (1)
$e + 3f = 13$ (2)

(e) $2m + n = 23$ (1)
$m + 4n = 22$ (2)

(f) $4p + q = 17$ (1)
$p - q = 3$ (2)

(g) $3s + r = 10$ (1)
$s - r = 2$ (2)

(h) $t + u = -1$ (1)
$u - t = -5$ (2)

(i) $2v + w = -6$ (1)
$v - w = -6$ (2)

(j) $2a - b = 4$ (1)
$6a - 5b = 18$ (2)

Solving simultaneous equations by elimination

In some cases, terms with a coefficient of 1 appear in neither equation and so it is not so easy to use substitution. Instead, it may be easier to use another algebraic method: elimination.

The elimination method relies on common terms appearing in both equations.

Elimination by subtraction

Common terms can be eliminated by *subtracting* one equation from the other.

Example

Find the values of a and b which solve this pair of simultaneous equations.

$4a + 2b = 26$ (1)

$2a + 2b = 16$ (2)

The term $2b$ is called a *common* term.

First, notice that the term $2b$ appears in both equations.

Here, subtracting Equation ② from Equation ① has the effect of eliminating b from the equations.

$$4a + 2b - (2a + 2b) = 26 - 16$$
$$4a + 2b - 2a - 2b = 10$$
$$2a = 10$$
$$a = 5$$

Having found a value for a, substitute this value into one of the equations and solve it to find the value of b.

$$2a + 2b = 16 \quad ②$$
$$2 \times 5 + 2b = 16$$
$$10 + 2b = 16$$
$$2b = 6$$
$$b = 3$$

Now, to check these two values, substitute $a = 5$ and $b = 3$ into the other equation.

$$4a + 2b \quad = 26 \quad ①$$
$$4 \times 5 + 2 \times 3 = 20 + 6 = 26 ✓$$

Always check your answers by substituting values back into the equations.

Elimination by addition

If two terms have the same coefficient but different signs, *adding* the two equations will eliminate these terms.

Example

3 is the coefficient of t in the term $3t$.

$$s + 3t = 19 \quad ①$$
$$2s - 3t = 11 \quad ②$$

Adding ① and ② gives

$$s + 3t + (2s - 3t) = 19 + 11$$
$$s + 3t + 2s - 3t = 30$$
$$3s = 30$$
$$s = 10$$

Now, substituting this value of s into Equation ① gives

$$s + 3t = 19 \quad ①$$
$$10 + 3t = 19$$
$$3t = 9$$
$$t = 3$$

Finally, to check these two values work for the other equation, substitute $s = 10$ and $t = 3$ into Equation ②

$$2s - 3t = 11 \quad ②$$
$$2 \times 10 - 3 \times 3 = 20 - 9 = 11 ✓$$

Exercise 4

Look for terms that are the same in both equations.

1 Use the elimination method to solve these pairs of simultaneous equations.

(a) $6x + y = 18$
$x + y = 8$

(b) $n + 8m = 26$
$n + m = 5$

(c) $3e + f = 17$
$2e + f = 13$

(d) $a + 3b = 12$
$a + 2b = 10$

(e) $2a + b = 7$
$a + b = 4$

(f) $5s + r = 21$
$2s + r = 12$

(g) $v + 6u = 31$
$v + u = 6$

(h) $5m + n = 27$
$m + n = 7$

Label the equations so that you can explain your working clearly.

2 Solve these pairs of simultaneous equations, eliminating one variable by adding the equations together.

(a) $3x + y = 10$
$x - y = 2$

(b) $2n + m = 8$
$n - m = 1$

(c) $2a - b = 13$
$a + b = 11$

(d) $3e + f = 3$
$2e - f = 1$

(e) $3q - r = 7$
$2q + r = 8$

(f) $2d - c = 10$
$3d + c = 25$

(g) $4a - b = 9$
$3a + b = 5$

(h) $2a + b = 10$
$a - b = 8$

(i) $5s + r = 8$
$3s - r = 4$

(j) $6u - v = 7$
$v - u = -2$

(k) $5m - n = \frac{1}{2}$
$m + n = 2\frac{1}{2}$

(l) $10x + y = 3\frac{1}{2}$
$8x - y = 1$

3 Eliminate a variable to solve these pairs of equations.

Decide whether you should add or subtract these equations to eliminate one of the variables.

(a) $2x + 3y = 14$
$3x + 3y = 18$

(b) $2a + 3b = 22$
$2a + b = 14$

(c) $5t + 4r = 43$
$5t + 2r = 29$

(d) $x + 4y = 4$
$5x - 4y = 14$

(e) $7x + 2z = 37$
$7x + z = 29$

(f) $9a + 2b = 3$
$6a - 2b = 2$

(g) $2v + 5w = 19$
$2v + 3w = 13$

(h) $12a + 13b = 76$
$7a + 13b = 66$

(i) $5m + 4n = 6$
$3m + 4n = 2$

(j) $2r + p = \frac{1}{2}$
$5r - p = 3$

(k) $5a + 3b = 20$
$5a + 4b = 25$

(l) $2x + 3y = 7$
$5x - 3y = 7$

(m) $f + g = 18$
$g - f = 12$

(n) $8d - 3c = 13$
$4d + 3c = 11$

Check your results by substituting your solutions back into the equations.

Making common terms for elimination

Common terms can be eliminated from a pair of simultaneous equations by simply adding or subtracting the two equations.

If a pair of equations has no common terms, multiplying one (or both) of the equations can produce two new simultaneous equations that *can* be solved using elimination.

Example

In these two equations, no two terms have the same coefficients.

$2a + 5b = 24$ ①

$4a + 3b = 20$ ②

To eliminate a from both equations, the coefficients have to be the same.

Multiplying all the terms in Equation ① by 2 gives:

$2 \times 2a + 2 \times 5b = 2 \times 24$

$4a + 10b = 48$

> **$2a$ is a factor of $4a$.**
> $2 \times 2a = 4a$

Label this new equation as ③

$4a + 10b = 48$ ③

Now, in Equations ② and ③, the terms in a are the same, so subtracting Equation ③ from Equation ② will eliminate the terms in a.

$4a + 3b = 20$ ②

$4a + 10b = 48$ ③

$$4a + 10b - (4a + 3b) = 48 - 20$$
$$4a + 10b - 4a - 3b = 28$$
$$7b = 28$$
$$b = 4$$

Substituting $b = 4$ back into Equation ②

$$4a + 3b = 20$$
$$4a + 3 \times 4 = 20$$
$$4a + 12 = 20$$
$$4a = 8$$
$$a = 2$$

Finally, to check these two values work for the other equation, substitute $a = 2$ and $b = 4$ into Equation ③

$4a + 10b = 48$ ③

$4 \times 2 + 10 \times 4 = 8 + 40 = 48$ ✓

> **Always check your answers by substituting values back into the equations.**

Example

In this example, none of the terms are factors of other terms.

It may necessary to multiply *both* equations.

$2x + 7y = 17$ ①

$5x - 3y = 22$ ②

Multiplying Equation ① by 5 and Equation ② by 2 eliminates the x terms.

5 × ①	$10x + 35y = 85$	③
2 × ②	$10x - 6y = 44$	④
③ – ④	$41y = 41$	
	$y = 1$	

Alternatively, multiplying ① by 3 and ② by 7 eliminates the y terms.

Substituting $y = 1$ back into Equation ① gives:

$2x + 7y = 17$ ①

$2x + 7 \times 1 = 17$

$2x + 7 = 17$

$2x = 10$

$x = 5$

Finally, to check these two values work for the other equation, substitute $x = 5$ and $y = 1$ into Equation ②.

$5x - 3y = 22$ ②

$5 \times 5 - 3 \times 1 = 25 - 3 = 22$ ✓

Exercise 5

Label the equations so that you can explain your working clearly.

1 Solve these pairs of simultaneous equations using an appropriate method.

(a) $2a + b = 8$
$3a - 2b = 5$

(b) $3c + 6d = 9$
$c + 8d = 6$

(c) $5m - 3n = 13$
$7m - n = 15$

(d) $3p + 2q = 8$
$5p + 3q = 13$

(e) $7h - 2j = 11$
$12h + 5j = 2$

(f) $6x + 7y = 13$
$3x - 2y = 1$

(g) $6j - 8k = 6$
$9j - 2k = 4$

(h) $10a + 2b = 11$
$5a - 6b = 2$

(i) $4r + 3s = 5$
$10r - 2s = 3$

(j) $11u - 3v = -13$
$9u + 4v = -30$

(k) $9x - 6y = 6$
$6x + 2y = 1$

(l) $5s - 7p = 27$
$3s - 4p = 16$

(m) $m + 5n = \frac{1}{2}$
$m - 3n = -3\frac{1}{2}$

(n) $a + 8b = 2\frac{1}{2}$
$2a - 4b = 0$

(o) $2f + 5g = 3$
$f - 5g = 6$

(p) $4b + 2c = 4$
$3b + 4c = 6$

(q) $p + 5q = 0$
$p + 3q = 0.1$

(r) $3v + w = -7$
$v + 2w = -6$

Exercise 6

1 Solve each of these problems by forming and solving a pair of simultaneous equations.

(a) Find the value of two numbers if their sum is 25 and their difference is 11.

(b) Two values are added to give 11. The difference between them is 1.

(c) The sum of two numbers is 1 and their difference is 7.

2 A collector buys 50 cards from Series I and 20 cards from Series II for £11. Another collector buys 30 cards from Series I and 40 from Series II for £15. Find the cost of cards from each series.

3 A school play was performed for two nights. On the first night, they sold 30 children's tickets and 70 adult tickets and received £220. On the second night, they sold 25 children's tickets and 90 adult tickets and raised £262.50. How much did each ticket cost?

Exercise 7

Label the equations so that you can explain your working clearly.

1 Solve these simultaneous equations by the method of substitution.

(a) $a = b + 6$
$b + a = 14$

(b) $y = 2x + 4$
$y - x = 7$

(c) $5m - n = 4$
$m + 2n = 3$

2 Solve these simultaneous equations using an appropriate method.

(a) $2a + b = 7$
$3a - b = 8$

(b) $4x + 2y = 34$
$3x - 2y = 15$

(c) $4m + 3n = 5$
$2m + 3n = 1$

(d) $4p + 2r = 8$
$p + 3r = 2$

(e) $\frac{1}{2}a - 3b = 6$
$3a - 5b = 23$

(f) $7x - 4y = 37$
$6x + 3y = 51$

3 Form simultaneous equations for each of these problems and solve them.

(a) The week's wages' bill for the supervisor and five workers is £1575. In the next week, the wages' bill is £1825 for the supervisor and six workers. Calculate the wages of the supervisor and the workers.

(b) A sales representative travels two hours at x mph and half an hour at y mph. She travels 110 miles. On another trip, she travels for one hour at x mph and two hours at y mph and travels 160 miles.
What values do x and y represent?

4 (a) Rearrange these pairs of simultaneous equations and solve them by drawing graphs.

(i) $2x - y = 1$
$x - y = -2$

(ii) $x - y = -1$
$x - 2y = -6$

(b) Use the most appropriate method to solve these equations to check your solutions to part (a).

Assignment 1 Polygon patterns

Look at this sequence of dots.

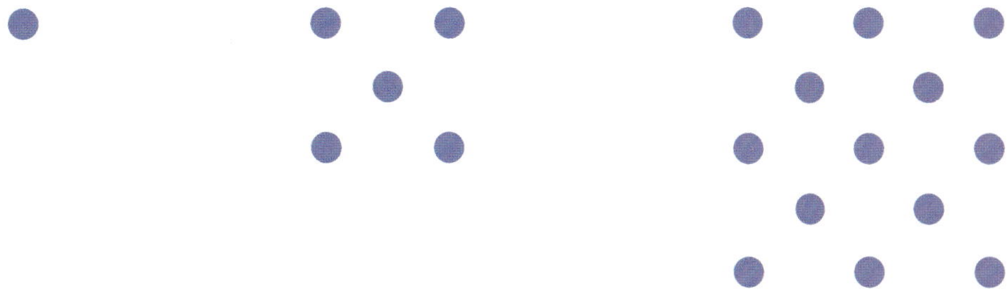

The number of dots in each diagram is given by this sequence.

Term (n)	1	2	3	4
Number of dots	1	5	13	—

The sequence is generated by this formula.

$an^2 + bn + 1$

When $n = 2$, the number of dots is 5, so

$5 = a \times 2^2 + b \times 2 + 1$

This equation can be rearranged as

$4a + 2b = 4$

- How many dots are there when $n = 3$?
  Form an equation using $n = 3$.
- You now have two equations in a and b.
  Solve these simultaneously equations to find a and b.
- Use the information gained by solving the simultaneous equations to continue the sequence to the tenth term.

What are my chances?

In this chapter you will learn:

- → **how to draw a probability tree diagram**
- → **how to calculate probabilities using a tree diagram**
- → **about the probability of mutually exclusive events**
- → **about the probability of independent events.**

Starting points

Before starting this chapter, you will need to be able to:

- find the probability of a single event
- add and multiply simple fractions
- understand that the total probability is always 1.

Exercise 1

1 A number is selected at random from this set of numbers.

1 2 3 4 5 6 7 8 9 10 11 12 13 14 15

(a) What is the probability that the number selected is even?

(b) What is the probability that the number selected is a multiple of 3?

(c) What is the probability that the number selected is neither even nor a multiple of 3?

2 Add together these fractions.

(a) $\frac{2}{7} + \frac{3}{7}$ (b) $\frac{1}{6} + \frac{1}{2}$ (c) $\frac{1}{4} + \frac{5}{12}$

3 Calculate these.

(a) $1 - \frac{2}{7}$ (b) $1 - \frac{4}{5}$ (c) $1 - \frac{2}{9}$

4 Multiply these fractions.

(a) $\frac{1}{2} \times \frac{2}{3}$ (b) $\frac{1}{5} \times \frac{2}{5}$ (c) $\frac{1}{6} \times \frac{5}{6}$

(d) $\frac{1}{7} \times \frac{1}{4}$ (e) $\frac{2}{9} \times \frac{1}{3}$ (f) $\frac{3}{5} \times \frac{3}{4}$

5 A box contains white tiles and patterned tiles. If the probability of choosing a white tile from the box is $\frac{7}{12}$, what is the probability of choosing a patterned tile?

6 If the probability of scoring 8 with two dice is $\frac{5}{36}$, what is the probability of *not* scoring 8?

7 If a packet of sweets contains six red, seven yellow and eight green sweets, what is the probability of choosing a red sweet from the packet?

Tree diagrams

In a board game, a fair dice is thrown for each go, but you need to throw a six to start. Each time the dice is thrown, two events are possible: either 'a six' or 'not a six'. Each throw of the dice can be shown on a diagram, like this.

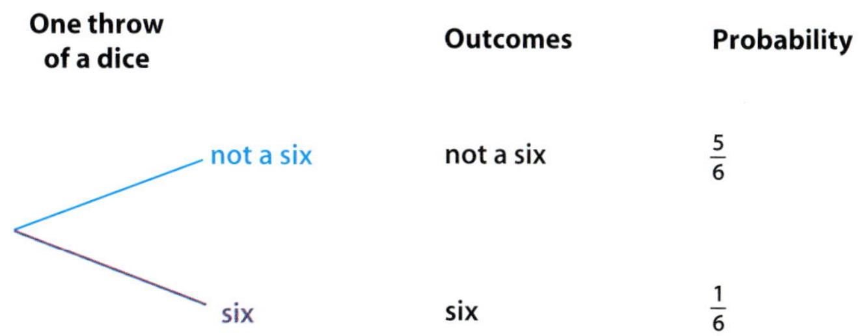

Because there are two possible outcome for each throw – 'a six' or 'not a six' – there are two branches for every throw.

The diagram can be extended to show the second throw of the dice, like this.

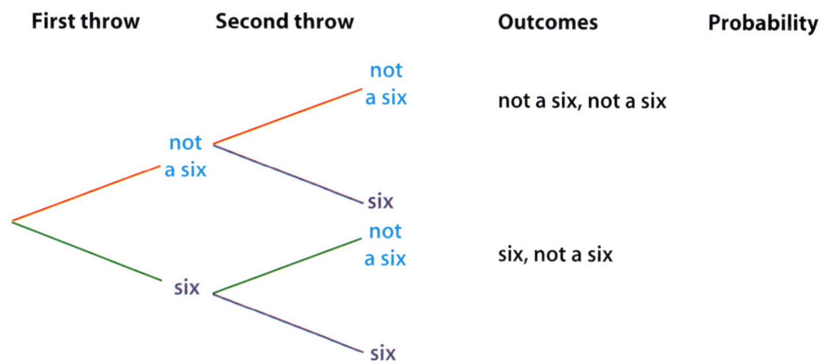

In this tree diagram, the green line shows two throws, 'a six' followed by 'not a six'. The red line shows 'not a six' followed by another 'not a six'.

Key fact

A tree diagram is used to represent events in probability.

This type of diagram is known as a 'tree diagram'. Here is the complete tree showing all possible outcomes of two throws.

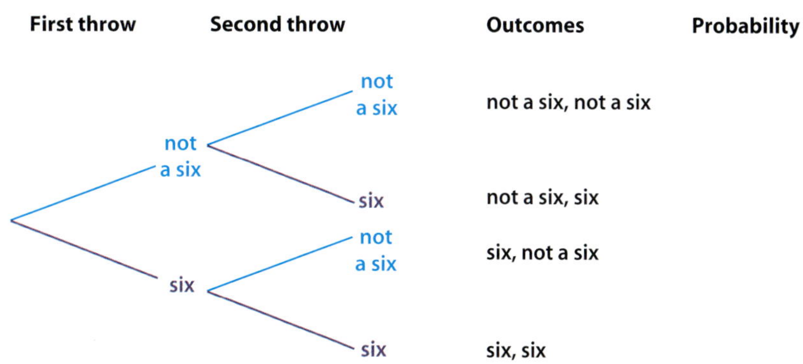

The diagram can be extended to show more than two throws.

Assignment 1 Three throws of a dice

- Copy the tree diagram for two throws of a dice and extend it to include a third throw.

> **Allow plenty of room for your diagram.**

- On your diagram, colour the branches which represent the three throws: 'six', 'six', 'six'.
- Which branches represent the three throws: 'not a six', 'not a six', 'not a six'?
- Find a branch that represents throwing two 'sixes' and one 'not a six'.

  Are there any other branches that show this outcome?

  How many routes are there altogether for two 'sixes' and one 'not a six'?
- How many routes are there altogether for throwing one 'six' and two 'not a six'?
- How many possible routes are there altogether?
- Draw an outcomes and probability table to record all possible outcomes.

Exercise 2

1 An unbiased coin is tossed twice.
Copy and complete this tree diagram and the table beside it to show all possible outcomes.

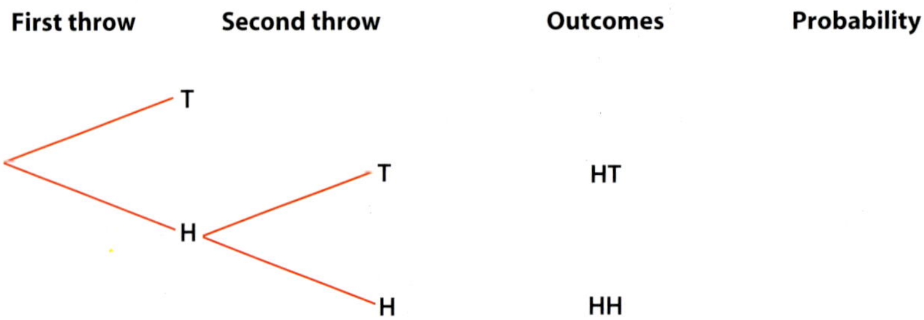

How many different ways are there of throwing:

(a) two heads?

(b) one head?

(c) no heads?

2 Draw a new tree diagram to show three throws of the coin and make a list of the different outcomes.

Write down the number of ways you can obtain three heads, two heads, one head and no heads with three throws.

3 By drawing a new diagram, or extending your previous one, make a list of all the different outcomes of throwing the coin four times.

Write down the number of ways of obtaining four heads, three heads, two heads, one head and no heads from four throws.

Assignment 2 More throws

- Using your results from the previous exercise, arrange your answers in the form of tables as shown here.

1 throw	
1 head	**0 heads**
1	1

2 throws		
2 heads	**1 head**	**0 heads**
1		

3 throws			
3 heads	**2 heads**	**1 head**	**0 heads**

- Make a table to represent four throws.
- Look at the results and write them in the form of a triangle.

1   1

1   2   1

This triangle is known as Pascal's triangle.

- Can you complete the next row of the triangle for five throws?
  What about six and seven throws?
- Total the rows of the triangle horizontally.
  $1 + 1 = 2$
  $1 + 2 + 1 = 4$
  $1 + 3 + 3 + 1 =$
  and so on.
- Write down anything you notice in the results.
- How many ways are there for eight throws?
  How many ways are there for ten throws?
  How many ways are there for twenty throws?
  What about *n* throws?

Calculating probabilities

If a dice is thrown twice, all possible outcomes can be shown on a possibility space.

1st throw (across), 2nd throw (down)

+	1	2	3	4	5	6
1	2	3	4	5	6	7
2	3	4	5	6	7	8
3	4	5	6	7	8	9
4	5	6	7	8	9	10
5	6	7	8	9	10	11
6	7	8	9	10	11	12

Outcomes	Probability
(six, six)	$\frac{1}{6} \times \frac{1}{6} = \frac{1}{36}$

The probability of throwing one six is $\frac{1}{6}$.
The diagram shows that the probability of throwing one six followed by another six is $\frac{1}{36}$.

Out of 36 outcomes, only one is a six and a six.

Key fact
P (A and B) $= P(A) \times P(B)$

$$P(\text{six}) = \frac{1}{6}$$

$$P(\text{six, six}) = P(\text{six}) \times P(\text{six}) = \frac{1}{6} \times \frac{1}{6} = \frac{1}{36}$$

If more throws of the dice are planned, a possibility space cannot be used to display all possible outcomes. Instead, you can use a tree diagram.

Calculating probabilities from a tree diagram

Each branch in a tree diagram can be labelled with the probability of that event occurring.

In the tree diagram used in Assignment 1, P(six) is the probability of throwing a six and

$$P(\text{six}) = \frac{1}{6}$$

$$P(\text{not a six}) = 1 - P(\text{six}) = \frac{5}{6}$$

From the diagram, the P(six) on the first throw is $\frac{1}{6}$. The P(six) on the second throw is also $\frac{1}{6}$ and again on the third.

To calculate the probability of throwing three sixes, P(six, six, six), the fractions are multiplied together.

$$P(\text{six, six, six}) = \frac{1}{6} \times \frac{1}{6} \times \frac{1}{6} = \frac{1}{216}$$

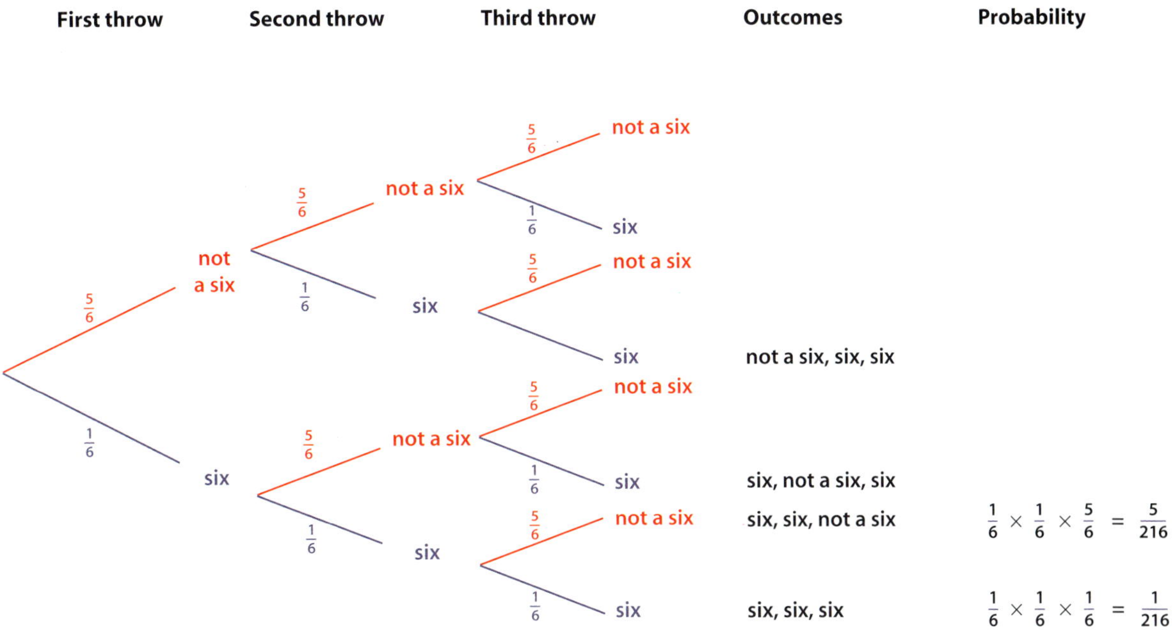

By looking at this diagram, you can see that, provided the order of obtaining a result is not important, the same result can come from more than one route. For two sixes and one 'not a six', the three routes are

six, six, not a six

six, not a six, six

not a six, six, six

The probability for each route is calculated by *multiplying* along the branches first, before the total probability is found by adding these probabilities together.

$$\text{P(two sixes and one 'not a six')} = \left(\frac{1}{6} \times \frac{1}{6} \times \frac{5}{6}\right) + \left(\frac{1}{6} \times \frac{5}{6} \times \frac{1}{6}\right) + \left(\frac{5}{6} \times \frac{1}{6} \times \frac{1}{6}\right)$$

$$= \frac{5}{216} + \frac{5}{216} + \frac{5}{216} = \frac{15}{216} = \frac{5}{72}$$

Assignment 3 Calculating probabilities from a tree diagram

The table on page 76 beside the tree diagram lists some of the outcomes of three throws of a dice.

- Copy and complete the tree diagram and the table to show all outcomes and probabilities.
- What is the total probability of all the outcomes?
- Write down each of the outcomes for throwing just one six from three throws.
- What is the probability for each route?
- Calculate the total probability for a 'six' from three throws.
- In how many outcomes do no sixes occur?
- Write down the probability of no sixes occurring.
- Using the results for throwing three, two, one and no sixes, calculate the total probability.

Exercise 3

1 In a game of darts, a player hits the bull's eye four times out of ten.

(a) What is the probability the player hits the bull's eye?
Write this probability as a fraction in its lowest terms.

(b) What is the probability the player does *not* hit the bull's eye?

(c) Draw a tree diagram for three attempts at hitting the bull's eye.
Calculate:

(i) the probability of hitting the bull's eye each time

(ii) the probability of hitting it two out of the three times.

2 The target is for an ambulance to arrive at the scene of an accident within 14 minutes of an emergency call being made.

These are the arrival times recorded for twenty accidents.

13, 12, 11, 12, 13, 17, 11, 10, 4, 15, 17, 12, 12, 9, 17, 18, 9, 10, 11, 13

(a) From this information, what is the probability the ambulance will arrive within the expected time?

(b) What is the probability that the ambulance arrives after more than 14 minutes?

(c) Draw a tree diagram and calculate the probability of it arriving within 14 minutes three times in a row.

(d) Calculate the probability of it arriving within 14 minutes for the first two occasions but not on the third.

(e) Calculate the probability it will arrive within 14 minutes two out of three times.

3 The probability of a frost at night in December is $\frac{1}{3}$.

(a) Draw a tree diagram to represent the nights 24th to 27th December inclusive.

(b) What is the probability it will be frosty every night?

(c) What is the chance it will be frosty on two out of the four nights?

4 The probability that the school bus arrives late is $\frac{1}{3}$.

(a) What is the probability that the school bus arrives on time?

(b) Draw a tree diagram to show the outcomes for three school days.

(c) Calculate the probability that the school bus will be late two out of three times.

(d) What is the probability that the school bus arrives on time for each of the three school days?

More tree diagrams

On some occasions, the probability of a second event is altered by the first event occurring. The events are no longer independent, and simply multiplying the starting probabilities does not give the correct result.

Example

One child has a packet of 25 sweets to eat.

The packet contains five red, seven green, eight yellow, two purple and three black sweets.

As one sweet is eaten there is going to be one less in the pack and the probability for choosing each colour changes.

Suppose that P(R) is the probability of picking a red sweet. Then, P(RR) can be shown on a tree diagram.

Include only those branches of the tree diagram that are relevant to the question.

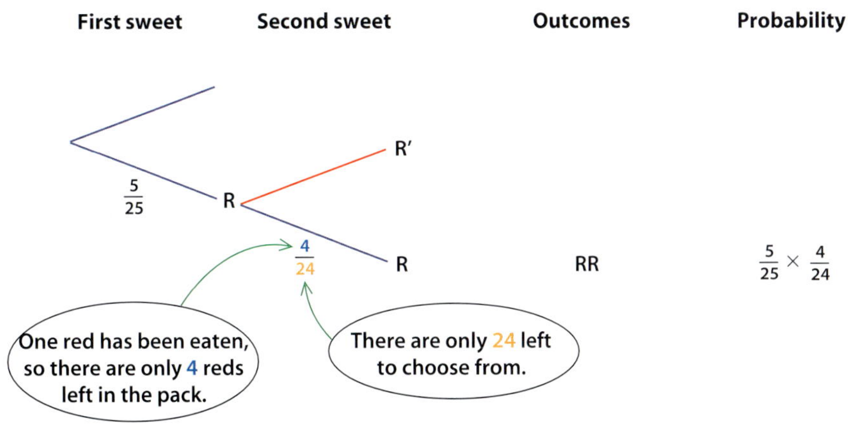

Similarly, the probability of choosing a purple followed by a black, P(PB) can be shown

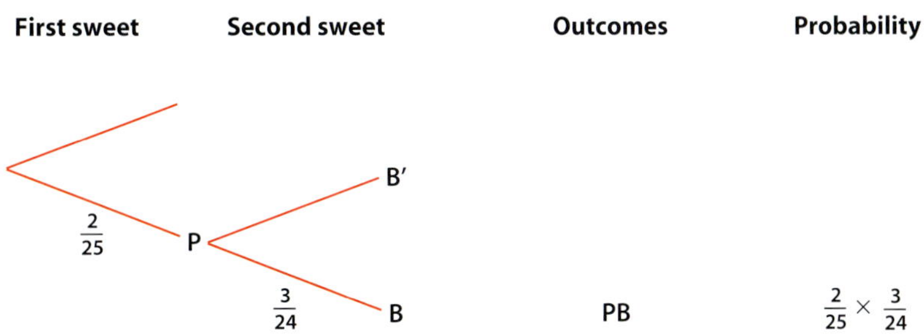

Exercise 4

1 Using a new packet of 25 sweets, calculate the probability of a child eating:

(a) a green sweet followed by another green sweet

(b) a yellow sweet followed by a green sweet

(c) a black sweet followed by a purple sweet.

2 For another new packet of 25 sweets, calculate:

(a) P(RG)

(b) P(GY)

(c) P(PG)

3 Another child picks out three sweets from a fresh packet of 25 sweets. Calculate the probability of that child picking:

(a) a black sweet, a purple sweet and a red sweet, in that order

(b) a red sweet, a purple sweet and a black sweet, in that order.

(c) Does the order matter?

4 Using another fresh packet of sweets, calculate these probabilities.

(a) P(BBG)

(b) P(BGY)

5 Four sweets are picked from another packet of 25 sweets. Find these probabilities.

(a) The probability of picking red, green, yellow, and black sweets

(b) The probability of picking green, yellow, yellow and black sweets

(c) P(RBBB)

6 A card is drawn from a pack of 52 playing cards and not replaced into the deck. This event is repeated three times.

(a) Draw a tree diagram to show the probability of drawing 'a heart' and 'not a heart'.

(b) What is the probability of drawing

(i) 3 hearts?

(ii) at least 2 hearts?

(iii) exactly one heart?

7 A pack of ten cards are numbered 1 to 10. One card is taken from the pack and not returned.

(a) What is the probability of drawing an even numbered card?

Three more cards are taken from the pack, and not returned. Four cards have now been drawn.

(b) What is the probability of drawing

(i) four even numbers?

(ii) at least three even numbers?

Independent events

If the result of one event affects the probability of later events, the later events are **dependent** on what happens earlier.

If an event can be repeated, and each time the probabilities remain the same, then the events are called **independent**.

Example

In a game of chance, there are three possible outcomes: win, lose or draw.
Each time the game is played, the probability of winning is $\frac{1}{3}$, the probability of losing is $\frac{1}{3}$ and so is that of a draw.

If two games are played, what is the probability of winning *both* the first game *and* the second game?

The key words here are 'both' and 'and'.

P(win game 1) = $\frac{1}{3}$

P(win game 2) = $\frac{1}{3}$

These two events are independent of one another.

P(A and B) = P(A) × P(B)

The probability of winning both games = $\frac{1}{3} \times \frac{1}{3}$

$= \frac{1}{9}$

Mutually exclusive events

Events are called mutually exclusive if they cannot both happen at the same time. One event happening excludes the possibility of the other event happening.

Example

A bag contains four red balls, two yellow balls and one green ball.

One ball is picked out of the bag.

What is the probability of picking *either* a red ball *or* a green ball?

The key words here are 'either' and 'or'.

P(red) = $\frac{4}{7}$

P(green) = $\frac{1}{7}$

If A and B are mutually exclusive events, probability of A or B = P(A) + P(B)

These two events are exclusive of one another, because you can either pick a red ball or pick a green ball, but a ball cannot be both red and green at the same time.

P(red or green) = $\frac{4}{7} + \frac{1}{7}$

$= \frac{5}{7}$

Exercise 5

1 A card is drawn from a pack of cards and a dice is thrown.

Event A is 'a Jack is drawn from the pack'.

Event B is 'a 3 is thrown with the dice'.

(a) Are A and B independent events?

(b) Are they mutually exclusive of one another?

(c) Write down the values of

(i) P(A)

(ii) P(B)

(iii) P(A or B)

(iv) P(A and B).

2 A card is drawn from a pack of cards.

Event X is 'a King is drawn'.

Event Y is 'a Queen is drawn'.

(a) Is event X independent of event Y?

(b) Are the two events mutually exclusive?

(c) Write down the values of

(i) P(X)

(ii) P(Y)

(iii) P(X or Y)

(iv) P(X and Y).

3 If a hedgehog tries to cross a certain road before 7.00 a.m., the probability of it being run over is $\frac{1}{10}$. After 7.00 a.m., the traffic is heavier and the probability of the hedgehog being run over increases to $\frac{3}{4}$.

The probability of the hedgehog waking up early enough to cross the road before 7.00 a.m. is $\frac{4}{5}$.

As soon as the hedgehog wakes up it tries to cross the road.

What is the probability of:

(a) the hedgehog waking up too late to cross the road before 7.00 a.m.?

(b) the hedgehog waking up early and crossing the road safely?

(c) the hedgehog waking up late and crossing the road safely?

(d) the hedgehog waking up early and being run over?

(e) the hedgehog crossing the road safely?

4 A sock is taken at random from a bag containing three red socks, four black socks and five green socks.

If each time one sock is taken out, its colour is noted and it is replaced, what is the probability of selecting

(a) two red socks?

(b) two green socks?

(c) one black sock and one green sock?

(d) two socks of the same colour?

5 The probability of a cat staying out at night is $\frac{3}{4}$.

If the cat stays in tonight, the probability of it staying out tomorrow night is $\frac{3}{8}$.

If the cat goes out tonight, the probability of it staying out tomorrow night is $\frac{1}{8}$.

(a) Draw a tree diagram to show all possible outcomes for tonight and tomorrow night.

(b) What is the probability of the cat staying out both nights?

(c) What is the probability that the cat will stay in for only one of the nights?

Assignment 4 Making a profit

A game at the local school fête is played with ten cards numbered 1 to 10.

Each person pays 10p and is dealt three different cards. If the sum of the numbers on their cards is more than 24, they win 50p.

- What would be the chances of winning?
- Would you consider this to be a good game to play?
- Alter the price, or the winning score, or the prize money, or all three, to make a different game.
- Is your game a fair game? Does the stallholder make a profit?

Quadratic curves

In this chapter you will learn:

- ➜ **how to construct a table of values for drawing curves**
- ➜ **how to draw curves**
- ➜ **how to recognise families of parabolas**
- ➜ **how to sketch curves.**

Starting points

Before starting this chapter, you will need to:

- know how to find a square number
- have access to a graphics calculator, or graphics program if possible.

Drawing curves

Assignment 1 Plotting the relationship between *x* and *y*

- Copy and complete this table of values.

x	0	1	2	3	4	5	6
y	0	1	4	9			

- What is the relationship between x and y?
- On a piece of A4 graph paper, draw the x axis about 2cm from the bottom of the page, with the origin in the centre.
  Use a scale of 1cm = 1 unit on the x axis, with values of x from -9 to $+9$.
  On the y axis, use 1cm = 4 units and include values up to 100.

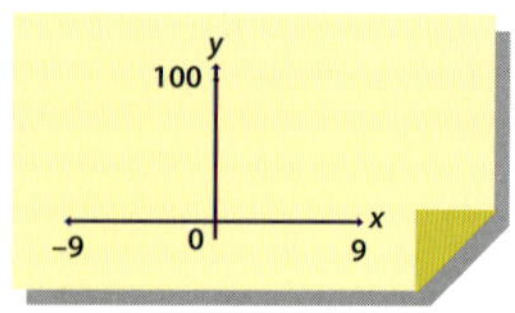

- Plot the points and join them with a smooth curve.
  Do *not* use a ruler to join the points.
- Reflect the curve in the y axis.
- What is the equation of the mirror line?
- What do you notice about the values of x for each value of y?
- Write an equation for the complete curve.
- From your graph, write down the value of 3.5^2.
- What two values are square roots of 64?
- Explain why there are two values of y for every value of x.

Exercise 1

1 Use your graph to evaluate these.

(a) $\sqrt{90}$ (b) 6.8^2 (c) $(-2.4)^2$

(d) $\sqrt{30}$ (e) $\sqrt{49}$ (f) $(-1)^2$

Parabolas

Key fact

The shape of the curve you have made is called a parabola.

The parabola was first studied by the Greeks. It is one of the conic sections, a shape which can be made by making a slice through a cone.

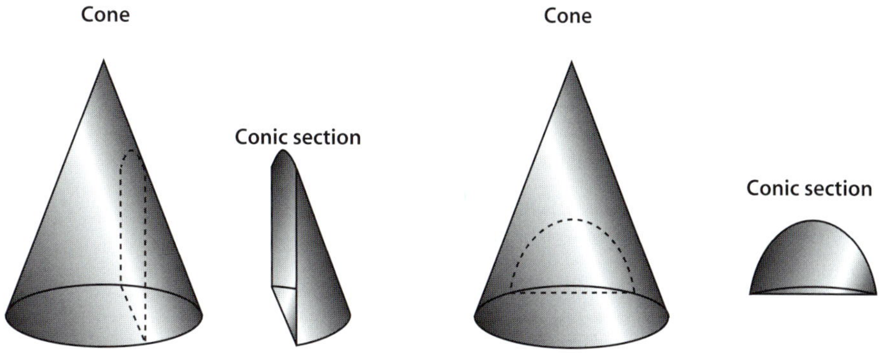

A fountain with jets of water coming out in many directions produces several parabolas; the outline of the water also produces a parabola.

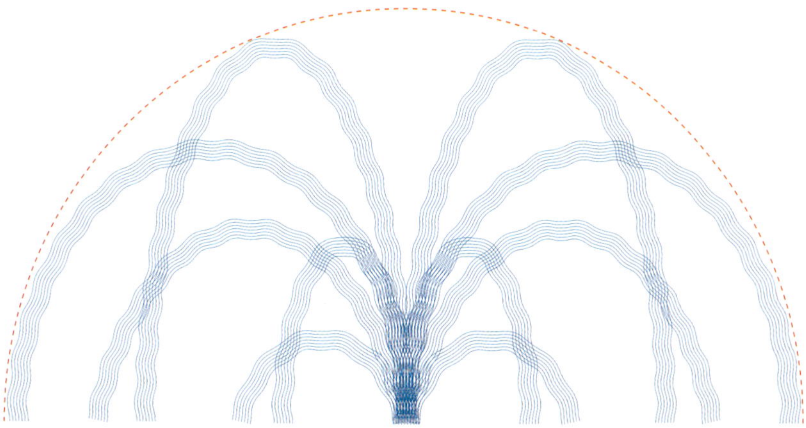

Assignment 2 Conic sections

- There are other conic sections. Find out about the other conic sections and draw them.
- Parabolas are used in a number of aspects of our lives. Find several examples of parabolas that can be seen in the environment.

Drawing graphs of parabolas

Assignment 3 Constructing a table of values

- Copy and complete this table of values for $y = x^2 + 2$.

x	−6	−5	−4	−3	−2	−1	0	1	2	3	4	5	6
x^2	36	25					0				16		
+2	+2	+2					+2				+2		
y	38	27					2				18		

- Draw axes with x taking values from −6 to + 6 and y taking values from −10 to 40. Plot the points and join them with a smooth curve. Where does this curve cut the y axis?
- On the same graph, sketch in the curve $y = x^2$ with a dotted line. What do you notice?
- Where would you expect the graph of $y = x^2 + 4$ to cut the y axis?
- Construct a table of values for $y = x^2 + 4$.
- Draw the graph of $y = x^2 + 4$ on the same graph and now put in $y = x^2 - 4$ *without* constructing a table of values.

Key fact

A coefficient is the number part of a term.
3 is the coefficient of x in the term $3x$.

Assignment 4 The family of parabolas

- Using either a graphics calculator (or a graphics program on the computer), investigate these graphs:

$y = 2x^2$ $\quad$ $y = 3x^2$ $\quad$ $y = \frac{1}{2}x^2$ $\quad$ $y = -x^2$

- Draw a sketch of each graph.
- What happens when the coefficient of x^2 changes.
- Which of the graphs is steepest?
- What do you notice if the coefficient of x^2 is a negative number?
- What do you notice about $y = x^2$ and $y = -x^2$?

Exercise 2

$y = -2x^2$
To calculate y when $x = -4$, square x first, then multiply by −2.
$-2 \times (-4)^2 = -2 \times +16$
$= -32$

1 (a) Calculate for $y = -2x^2$ the values of y when x is 0, −4, 3, 5, and −2.

(b) Copy and complete this table of values for $y = -2x^2$.

x	−4	−3	−2	−1	0	1	2	3	4
y	−32						−8		

(c) Draw the graph on A4 graph paper, extending your graph to fill the page.

(d) What are the values for x when $y = -40$, and $y = -20$?

(e) What is the value of y when $x = -3.5$? What is the value of y when $x = -1.5$?

2 Construct a table of values for $y = -\frac{1}{2}x^2$ and use the information to plot the graph.

Graphs with different coefficients of x^2

$y = 2x^2 + 4$

This can be shown in a flow diagram and values for y should be calculated in this order.

x → x^2 → $\times 2$ → $+4$ → $y = 2x^2 + 4$

When $x = -3$, this becomes

-3 → $-3 \times -3 = 9$ → $9 \times 2 = 18$ → $18 + 4 = 22$ → $y = 22$

This can be recorded in a table:

x	−3	−2	−1	0	1	2	3
x^2	9					4	
$2x^2$	18					8	
+4	+4					+4	
y	22					12	

Exercise 3

1 Copy and complete the table of values for $y = 2x^2 + 4$ with $-3 \leqslant x \leqslant 3$.

2 Draw a flow diagram for $y = 3x^2 - 2$.

Use your flow diagram to construct a table of values with $-3 \le x \le 4$ and draw the graph.

3 Construct a table of values for $y = 4x^2 - 2$ with $-3 \leqslant x \leqslant 4$ and draw the graph.

4 What do you notice about the graphs in Questions 2 and 3?

5 Draw the graph of $y = x^2 - 2$ without constructing a table of values.

Assignment 5 Drawing graphs of $y = (x + b)^2$

For $y = (x + 2)^2$, for example, the values of y can again be recorded in a table.

x	−3	−2	−1	0	1	2	3	4	5
$x + 2$	−1	0	1	2					7
$(x + 2)^2$	1	0	1	4					49

- Copy and complete this table of values.
- On an A4 piece of graph paper, draw axes with x taking values from −9 to 9 and y taking values from −2 to 50.
- Plot the points and join them with a smooth curve.
  Mark points for y when x is −4, −5, −6, −7, −8 and join with a dotted curve, or using a coloured pencil.
- What is the value of x when $y = 0$?
- What do you notice about this value of x and the equation?
- Where does the curve cut the y axis?
- What do you notice about this value and the equation?

A parabola has a line of symmetry.

Exercise 4

1 (a) Construct a table of values for $y = (x + 4)^2$ for $-6 \leqslant x \leqslant 6$.
(b) Plot on the same axes as those used in Assignment 6.
(c) When $x = 0$, what is the value of y?
(d) What is the value of x when $y = 0$?

2 (a) Construct a table of values for $y = (x - 3)^2$.
(b) On the same axis as before draw the graph for $-3 \leqslant x \leqslant 6$.
(c) What do you notice?

3 (a) Where would you expect the graph of $y = (x - 5)^2$ to cut the y axis?
(b) Where would you expect the line of symmetry to be?
(c) Where would the graph cut the x axis?
(d) Draw the graph of $y = (x - 5)^2$ *without* constructing a table of values.

Sketching graphs

To sketch a graph we need to know various things about the graph:

- the cutting point on the y axis, i.e. when $x = 0$
- the point(s) at which the curve cuts the x axis, i.e. when $y = 0$
- the curve to which it is similar.

To sketch $y = x^2 + 3$

Think

- The cutting point is at (0,3).
- The graph is similar to $y = x^2$ which is symmetrical about the y axis.

It is often a good idea to put in $y = x^2$ with a dotted line.

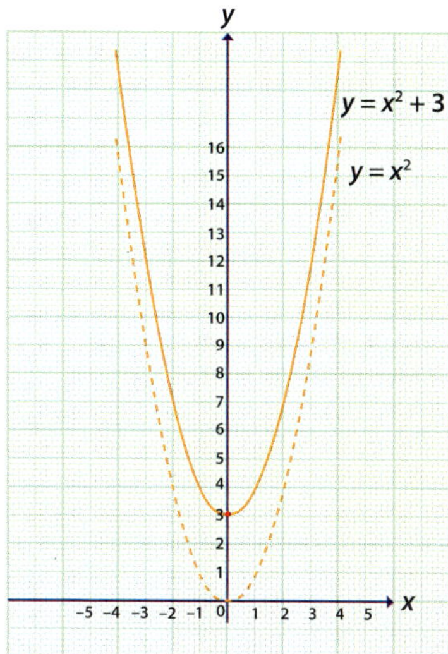

Any graph like $y = x^2$ can be sketched but you must remember that the curves do not remain parallel. They are closer together 'at the ends'.

You must label the axes and show the intercept.

To sketch graphs like $y = (x + 3)^2$

Think

When $x = 0$
$y = (0 + 3)^2 = 9$

- The graph cuts the y axis when $x = 0$ and $y = 9$
- The graph cuts the x axis when $y = 0$ and $x = -3$
- The graph is similar to $y = x^2$ but is shifted along the x axis.

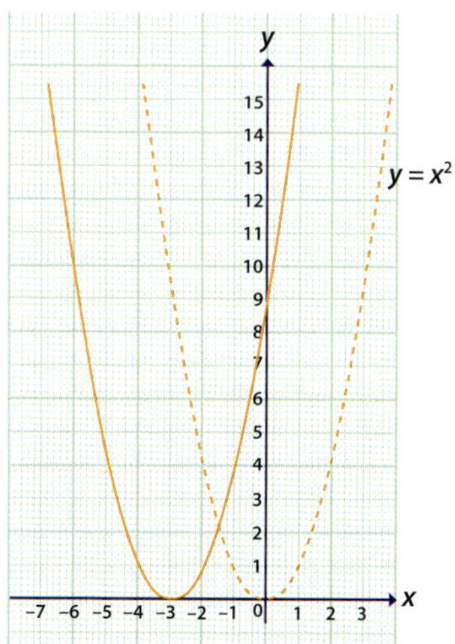

To sketch curves with different coefficients of x^2

Example

$y = 2x^2 + 2$

Think

- The graph cuts the y axis when $x = 0$, i.e. when $y = 2$.
- The graph is steeper than $y = x^2$, and the curve is narrower.

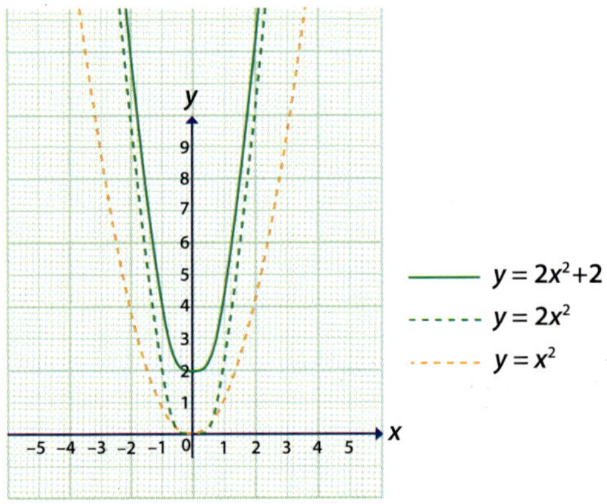

If the coefficient of x^2 is negative, the curve is the other way up.

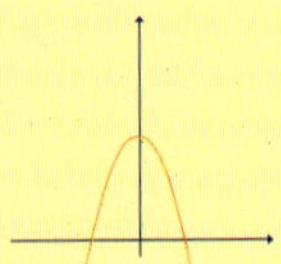

Exercise 5

1 Sketch these graphs.

(a) $y = x^2$ (b) $y = x^2 - 2$ (c) $y = 2x^2$

(d) $y = -x^2 + 3$ (e) $y = (x - 1)^2$ (f) $y = (x + 5)^2$

(g) $y = -2x^2 + 3$ (h) $y = \frac{1}{2}x^2$ (i) $y = -\frac{1}{2}x^2 + 5$

2 Write down the equation of these curves.

(a)

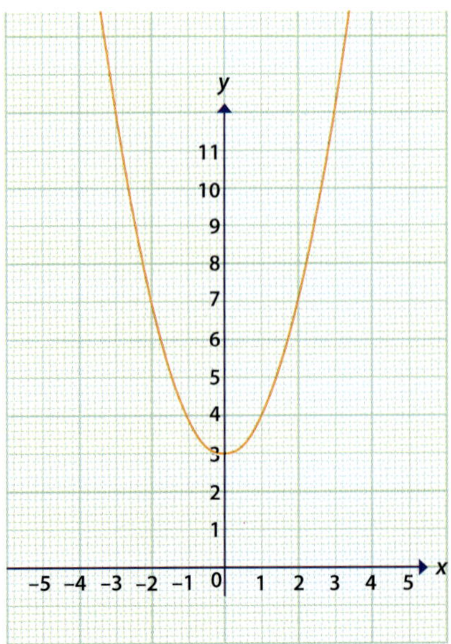

(b)

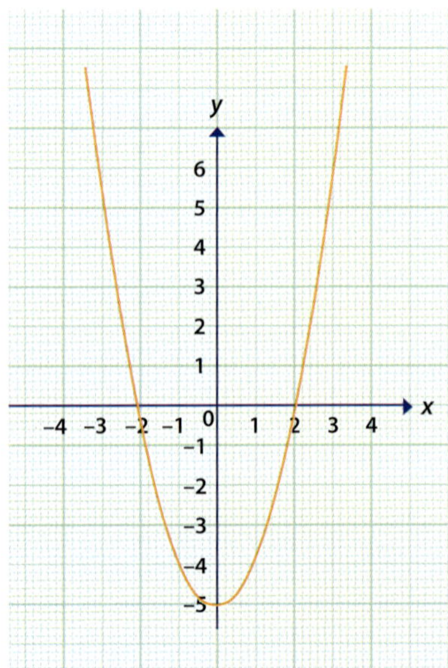

(c)

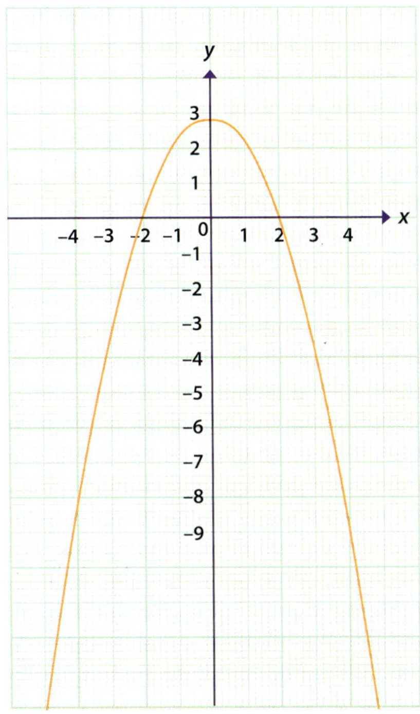
y
x
3
2
1
–4 –3 –2 –1 0 1 2 3 4
–1
–2
–3
–4
–5
–6
–7
–8
–9

(d)

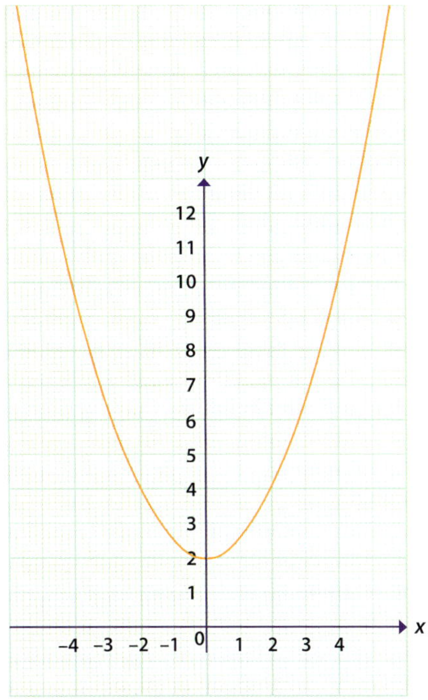
y
x
12
11
10
9
8
7
6
5
4
3
2
1
–4 –3 –2 –1 0 1 2 3 4

(e)

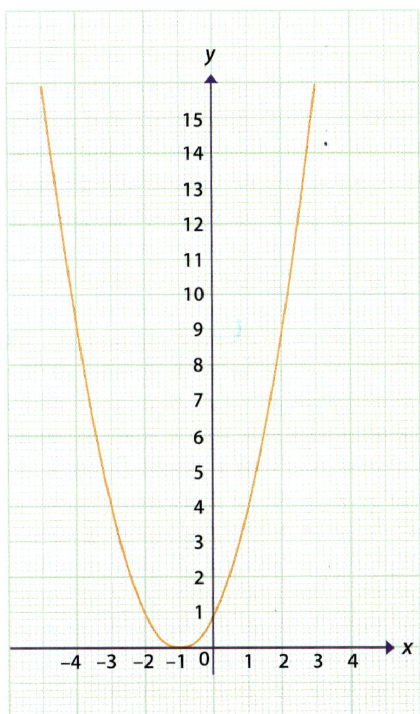
y
x
15
14
13
12
11
10
9
8
7
6
5
4
3
2
1
–4 –3 –2 –1 0 1 2 3 4

(f)

y
x
15
14
13
12
11
10
9
8
7
6
5
4
3
2
1
0 1 2 3 4 5 6 7 8 9

Assignment 7 Investigating curves

- Using a graphics calculator (or a graphics program on the computer) investigate different curves by changing the powers of x, changing the coefficients of x^2 and x, and the constant term, e.g.

  $y = x^3$

  $y = x^4$

  $y = \frac{1}{2}x^3 - 3$

- What about curves like $y = x^2 + 4x + 4$ and $y = x^2 - 6x + 9$?
- What do you notice about these curves?
- What about $y = (x + 2)^2$ and $y = (x - 3)^2$?
- Can you see a connection between $y = x^2 + 4x + 4$ and $y = (x + 2)^2$?
- What would the curve of $y = (x - 5)^2$ be the same as? Try some others.

Answers

Chapter 1

Exercise 1 p1

1 (a) 16 (b) 121 (c) 400
(d) 5 (e) 9 (f) 15
2 (a) 576 (b) 2.56 (c) 17
(d) 1.9 (e) 5.7 (f) 5.3
3 6.7
4 (a) 570 (b) 380
5 detached: 112; semi-detached: 224; bungalows: 168
6 (a) 42 (b) $\frac{1}{4}$
7 (a) £1.80 (b) £1.35 (c) $\frac{9}{16}$
8 (a) $\frac{1}{4}$ (b) $\frac{1}{25}$ (c) $\frac{9}{16}$
(d) $\frac{4}{9}$ (e) $\frac{1}{100}$ (f) $\frac{1}{10000}$
9 (a) $\frac{1}{5}$ (b) $\frac{1}{3}$ (c) $\frac{1}{6}$
(d) $\frac{2}{3}$ (e) $\frac{2}{5}$ (f) $\frac{7}{8}$

Assignment 1 Building a multiplication table p2

×	-4	-3	-2	-1	0	1	2	3	4
4	-16	-9	-8	-4	0	4	8	12	16
3	-12	-9	-6	-3	0	3	6	9	12
2	-8	-6	-4	-2	0	2	4	6	8
1	-4	-3	-2	-1	0	1	2	3	4
0	0	0	0	0	0	0	0	0	0
-1	4	3	2	1	0	-1	-2	-3	-4
-2	8	6	4	2	0	-2	-4	-6	-8
-3	12	9	6	3	0	-3	-6	-9	-12
-4	16	12	8	4	0	-4	-8	-12	-16

Exercise 2 p3

1 (a) −3 (b) −8 (c) −9 (d) 8
(e) 0 (f) 12 (g) 9 (h) 16
(i) 4
2 (a) 3 (b) 4 (c) 3 (d) 0
3 (a) 3 (b) −3 (c) −4 (d) −8
(e) 4 (f) 4 (g) 0 (h) 1
5 (a) −21 (b) 32 (c) −30 (d) 100
(e) −40 (f) −4 (g) −4 (h) 4
(i) −3 (j) 0 (k) 9 (l) −600
6 (a) −50 (b) 6 (c) 6 (d) −40
(e) 0 (f) −10 (g) −16 (h) 32
7 (a) 5 (b) −12 (c) −3 (d) 7
(e) 0 (f) 2 (g) 5 (h) −100
8 (a) −3 (b) 2 (c) −9 (d) 0
(e) −3 (f) 14 (g) 7 (h) 5
9 (a) 36 (b) 25 (c) 49 (d) 64
(e) 9 (f) 100 (g) 1600 (h) −225
10 (a) +5 or −5 (b) +10 or −10 (c) +1 or −1
11 (a) −18 (b) 30 (c) −4 (d) 5
(e) −35 (f) 9 (g) −8 (h) $\frac{1}{8}$
(i) 144 (j) $\frac{1}{4}$ (k) $\frac{1}{16}$ (l) $\frac{9}{16}$

Exercise 3 p4

1 (a)

Length of side l (cm)	0	1	2	3	4	5	6	7	8
Volume of cube V (cm^3)	0	1	8	27	64	125	216	343	512

(b)

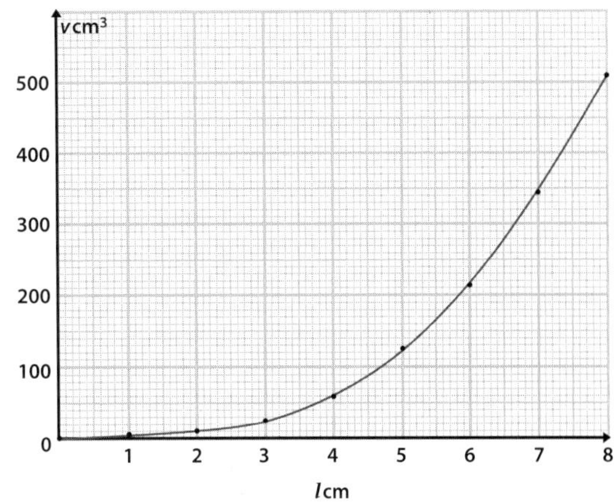

(c) 91.1 (d) 6.9 (e) $\sqrt[3]{325}$ is approximately 6.9
2 (a) 1728 (b) 3375 (c) 5832 (d) 15.625
(e) $\frac{1}{8}$ (f) $\frac{1}{1000}$ (g) $\frac{8}{125}$ (h) 0
3 (a) 4 (b) 5 (c) 6 (d) 10
(e) $\frac{1}{3}$ (f) $\frac{1}{2}$ (g) $\frac{1}{10}$ (h) $\frac{3}{5}$
4 $\sqrt[3]{8} = 2$; $\sqrt[3]{27} = 3$; $\sqrt[3]{12} = 2.3$ to 1 d.p.
5 (a) −27 (b) −125 (c) −216 (d) −343
(e) −16 (f) −1 (g) −512 (h) −1000
6 (a) −2 (b) −5 (c) −1 (c) −3

Assignment 2 Building pyramids p5

64 cubes make a pyramid with eight layers; 4 layers

For n layers, number of blocks $= 1^2 + 2^2 + 3^2 + \cdots + n^2$

$= \frac{1}{6}n(n+1)(2n+1)$

Assignment 3 Folding p6

The maximum number of folds is seven irrespective of the thickness of paper used.

$s = 2^x$

Exercise 4 p6

1 (a) 2^4 (b) 5^3 (c) 8^7
(d) 10^4 (e) 2.1^3 (f) 20^5

2 (a) $2^3 \times 3^4$ (b) $4^2 \times 5^3$ (c) $6^3 \times 7^4 \times 2^2$
(d) $2^3 \times 3^2 \times 5^2$ (e) $2 \times 6^3 \times 7^2$ (f) $2^7 \times 3 \times 5$

3 (a) 25 (b) 256 (c) 81
(d) 1296 (e) 1000000 (f) 256
(g) $\frac{1}{16}$ (h) $\frac{1}{125}$ (i) $\frac{16}{81}$

4 (a) 108 (b) 1600 (c) 1000
(d) 490000 (e) 2 (f) 1

5 (a) 4 (b) 3 (c) 4
(d) 5 (e) 4 (f) 3

6 (a) (b) $2^3 = 8$

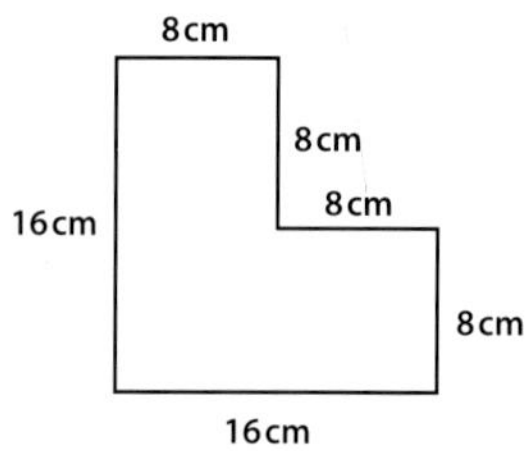

7 (a) 56 (b) 1/8

Assignment 4 Sequences p8

Sequence	Written as powers	Behaviour as *n* increases
2, 4, 8, 16, …	$2^1, 2^2, 2^3, \ldots, 2^n$	Diverges
5, 25, 125, …	$5^1, 5^2, 5^3, \ldots, 5^n$	Diverges
10, 100,1000, …	$10^1, 10^2, 10^3, \ldots, 10^n$	Diverges
0.1, 0.01, 0.001, …	$(0.1)^1, (0.1)^2, (0.1)^3, \ldots, (0.1)^n$	Converges
$\frac{1}{2}, \frac{1}{4}, \frac{1}{8}, \ldots$	$(\frac{1}{2})^1, (\frac{1}{2})^2, (\frac{1}{2})^3, \ldots, (\frac{1}{2})^n$	Converges
$\frac{1}{3}, \frac{1}{9}, \frac{1}{27}, \ldots$	$(\frac{1}{3})^1, (\frac{1}{3})^2, (\frac{1}{3})^3, \ldots, (\frac{1}{3})^n$	Converges

Exercise 5 p8

1 (a) 729 (b) 1331 (c) 5832
(d) 17.576 (e) 1.728 (f) 0.343

2 (a) 4096 (b) 78125 (c) 14641
(d) 0.03125 (e) 19683 (f) 46656

3 (a) 8 (b) 21 (c) 16

4 (a) 8192 (b) 30625 (c) 41472
(d) 8.192 (e) 2 160 000 (f) 2916
(g) 77.76 (h) 237304.6875 (i) 2.56

Exercise 6 p9

1 (a) 2^7 (b) 5^6 (c) 8^7
(d) 10^6 (e) 3^9 (f) 4^7
(g) 7^9 (h) $(\frac{1}{2})^9$ (i) $(0.1)^{15}$

2 (a) 6^2 (b) 5 (c) 13^3
(d) 10^2 (e) $3^0 = 1$ (f) 7^3
(g) $4^0 = 1$ (h) 3 (i) 5^{20}

3 (a) 4^6 (b) 5^6 (c) 2^9
(d) 7^{10} (e) 10^8 (f) 3^{12}
(g) $(\frac{1}{2})^6$ (h) $(\frac{1}{3})^6$ (i) 0.1^8

4 (a) $2^3 \times 3^9$ (b) $5^6 \times 7^2$ (c) $2^7 \times 4^7 = 2^{21}$

5 (a) 7^7 (b) 5^9 (c) $4^5 \times 5^4$

Exercise 7 p10

1 (a) $(-2)^5$ (b) $(-7)^3$ (c) $(-10)^4$ (d) $(-4)^3$

2 (a) –125 (b) 64 (c) –27 (d) –1
(e) 64 (f) 1000000 (g) 1 (h) –1000000

3 (a) –3125 (b) 729 (c) 20736 (d) –343
(e) 5.0625 (f) –13.824 (g) 0.49 (h) –0.000001

4 (a) $(-3)^6$ (b) $(-4)^7$ (c) $(-5)^7$ (d) $(-2)^9$
(e) $(-2)^{12}$ (f) $(-2)^{12}$ (g) $(-3)^6$ (h) $(-4)^4$
(i) $(-4)^2$ (j) –3 (k) $(-2)^6$ (l) –3

Assignment 5 Rules p10

$a^x \times a^y = a^{x+y}$ $a^x \div a^y = a^{x-y}$ $(a^x)^y = a^{xy}$

$a^0 = 1$ can be seen using the rule for division when a number is divided by itself, or the rule for multiplication when a number is multiplied by its reciprocal.

Assignment 6 Products p11

Maximum product is 20736 found in four squares:

Minimum product is zero.

The product of the four numbers in any 2-by-2 square is always a square number.

Exercise 8 p11

1 (a) 900 (b) 12 (c) $\frac{1}{5}$ (d) $\frac{4}{9}$

2 (a) 64 (b) $\frac{1}{8}$ (c) 0.001 (d) 0.125

3 (a) 10 (b) $\frac{1}{2}$ (c) $\frac{2}{3}$ (d) $\frac{5}{2}$

4 (a) 4 (b) –12 (c) –4 (d) 50
(e) 25 (f) 0 (g) –5 (h) 256

5 (a) 32 (b) 10000 (c) 144 (d) 500
(e) 6400000 (f) $\frac{1}{64}$ (g) –1 (h) 16

6 (a) 4 (b) 3 (c) 6
(d) 4 (e) 3 (f) 5

7 (a)

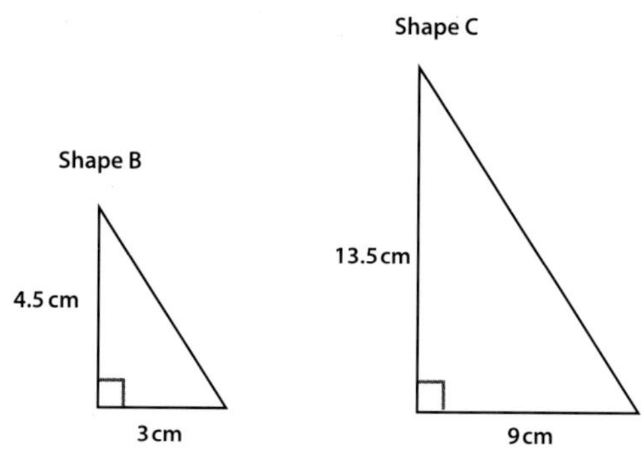

(b) $3^4 = 81$

8 (a) 1 (b) $(\frac{1}{4})^3 = \frac{1}{64}$

9 (a) 5^9 (b) 10^8 (c) $(-2)^5$
(d) 3^2 (e) 5^4 (f) 3^3
(g) -5 (h) $2^5 \times 3^2$ (i) $3^8 \times 5^2$

10 (a) 1728 (b) 17 (c) 32768
(d) 0.04 (e) 1296 (f) -9
(g) 65536 (h) 25.3125 (i) 432

Assignment 7 Prime factors p13

$30 = 2 \times 3 \times 5$ **$72 = 2 \times 2 \times 2 \times 3 \times 3 = 2^3 \times 3^2$**

$24 = 2^3 \times 3$ **$20 = 2^2 \times 5$**

HCF(20, 24) = 4

LCM(20, 24) = 120

Assignment 8 Powers of eleven p13

The values of 11^1, 11^2, 11^3, 11^4, are the second to fifth rows of Pascal's Triangle.

$11^5 = 161051$

$11^5 = 161051$

$11^6 = 1771561$

$11^7 = 19487171$

$11^8 = 214358881$

Chapter 2

Exercise 1 p14

1 (a) (i) 1, 2, 3, 4, 6, 8, 12, 24
(ii) 1, 2, 3, 6, 7, 14, 21, 42
(iii) 1, 2, 3, 6, 9, 18
(iv) 1, 2, 3, 4, 6, 9, 12, 18, 36
(v) 1, 29
(vi) 1, 2, 4, 5, 10, 20, 25, 50, 100
(vii) 1, 5, 25
(viii) 1, 2, 3, 4, 5, 6, 8, 10, 12, 15, 20, 24, 30, 40, 60, 120
(ix) 1, 37
(x) 1, 5, 17, 85
(xi) 1, 2, 3, 4, 6, 8, 9,12, 16, 18, 24, 36, 48, 72, 144
(xii) 1, 3, 37, 111

(b) 29, 37 They have exactly two factors: 1 and the number itself.

(c) 36, 100, 25, 144 They have an odd number of factors

2 (a) 1, 2, 3, 6 (b) 1, 5 (c) 1, 2, 5, 10
(d) 1, 2, 3, 4, 6, 12 (e) 1, 3, 13, 39 (f) 1, 2, 3, 4, 6, 12
(g) 1, 2, 17, 34 (h) 1, 19 (i) 1, 3, 7, 21

3 (a) 9 (b) 0 (c) 3
(d) 2 (e) 2 (f) 3

4 (a) 2 (b) -15 (c) -11 (d) -10
(e) 42 (f) 10 (g) -3 (h) -2
(i) 4 (j) -2 (k) 8 (l) -65

5 (a) (i) $3 + 2 \times (5 - 4) = 5$ (ii) $(3 + 2) \times 5 - 4 = 21$
(iii) $3 + 2 \times 5 - 4 = 9$ (iv) $(8 - 4) + 6 \div 2 = 7$
(v) $8 - ((4 + 6) \div 2) = 3$ (vi) $8 - (4 + 6 \div 2) = 1$

(b) $8 + 5 \times 4 - 7 = 21$ $(8 + 5) \times 4 - 7 = 45$
$8 + 5 \times (4 - 7) = -7$ $(8 + 5) \times (4 - 7) = -39$

6 (a) $3a + 2b$ (b) $4p + 2q$ (c) $2t$
(d) $5m + 3n$ (e) $w + t$ (f) $4x + 2y - 7z$

Exercise 2 p15

1 (a) $2a + 2b$ (b) $4s - 4t$ (c) $3p + 6q$
(d) $6m + 10n$ (e) $8v - 12t$ (f) $fg + fh$
(g) $3tw - dw$ (h) $2ek + 2eh$ (i) $6fm - 3gm$
(j) $3d^2 - 2de$ (k) $a^3 + a^2b$ (l) $4ks^2 - 8s^3$

2 (a) $5a + 5b$ (b) $3p + 7q$ (c) $8a + 14b$
(d) $5c + d$ (e) $22s + 7t$ (f) $8p - 14q$
(g) $x + y$ (h) p (i) $2d - 16e$
(j) $11a + 12b$ (k) $6d + 24e$ (l) f

3 (a) $a^2 + 5a + 6$ (b) $c^2 + 6c + 8$ (c) $p^2 + 10p + 25$
(d) $m^2 + 2m - 15$ (e) $2p^2 + 8p + 8$ (f) $6x^2 + 14x + 8$
(g) $6f^2 + 8f - 8$ (h) $p^2 - 5p + 6$ (i) $6g^2 - 23g + 20$
(j) $a^2 + 2ab + b^2$ (k) $a^2 - b^2$ (l) $2s^2 - 5st + 2t^2$

Exercise 3 p16

1 (a) 1, 2, c, $2c$ (b) 1, 3, a, $3a$
(c) 1, 2, 3, 6, d, $2d$, $3d$, $6d$
(d) 1, 2, b, c, $2b$, $2c$, bc, $2bc$
(e) 1, 2, 3, 4, 6, 12, f, $2f$, $3f$, $4f$, $6f$, $12f$, g, $2g$, $3g$, $4g$, $6g$, $12g$, fg, $2fg$, $3fg$, $4fg$, $6fg$, $12fg$
(f) 1, a, a^2 (g) 1, 3, m, $3m$, m^2, $3m^2$
(h) 1, 2, 4, 8, s, $2s$, $4s$, $8s$, s^2, $2s^2$, $4s^2$, $8s^2$
(i) 1, a, b, b^2, ab, ab^2
(j) 1, 2, 3, 6, f, $2f$, $3f$, $6f$, f^2, $2f^2$, $3f^2$, $6f^2$, g, $2g$, $3g$, $6g$, fg, $2fg$, $3fg$, $6fg$, f^2g, $2f^2g$, $3f^2g$, $6f^2g$
(k) 1, 2, 4, 8, 16, t, $2t$, $4t$, $8t$, $16t$, t^2, $2t^2$, $4t^2$, $8t^2$, $16t^2$, t^3, $2t^3$, $4t^3$, $8t^3$, $16t^3$
(l) 1, 3, d, $3d$, e, $3e$, e^2, $3e^2$, f, $3f$, de, $3de$, de^2, $3de^2$, df, $3df$, ef, $3ef$, e^2f, $3e^2f$, def, $3def$, de^2f, $3de^2f$

2 (a) 1, 2 (b) 1, a (c) 1, 3
(d) 1, 2, 4 (e) 1, 2, p, $2p$ (f) 1, m
(g) 1, 2, g, $2g$ (h) 1, 2, g, $2g$ (i) 1, x
(j) 1, 2, t, $2t$ (k) 1, t, t^2
(l) 1, 3, a, $3a$, b, $3b$, ab, $3ab$

3 (a) 2 (b) 2 (c) d (d) $2a$
(e) $4q$ (f) $2st$ (g) $5r$ (h) $3b$
(i) a^2 (j) $3b^2$ (k) $2k$ (l) $2pq$

4 Expressions *not* crossed out should be
$2x + 4$, $\frac{1}{2}(4x + 8)$, $2(x + 2)$

5 (a)

	$x + 2$
2	$2x + 4$

$2(x + 2) = 2x + 4$

(b)

	$x + 2$
3	$3x + 6$

$3(x + 2) = 3x + 6$

(c)

	$2x + 3$
4	$8x + 12$

$4(2x + 3) = 8x + 12$

(d)

	$2x + 1$
3	$6x + 3$

$3(2x + 1) = 6x + 3$

(e)

	$2x - 3$
2	$4x - 6$

$2(2x - 3) = 4x - 6$

(f)

	$3x - 2$
2	$6x - 4$

$2(3x - 2) = 6x - 4$

6 (a) $3x + 6 = 3(x + 2)$ (b) $2x + 4 = 2(x + 2)$
(c) $4a + 8 = 4(a + 2)$ (d) $4d + 6 = 2(2d + 3)$
(e) $12g + 8 = 4(3g + 2)$ (f) $3a - 9 = 3(a - 3)$
(g) $8m - 6 = 2(4m - 3)$ (h) $8 - 4m = 4(2 - m)$
(i) $10 - 5t = 5(2 - t)$

7 (a)

	x $+3$
x	x^2+3x

$x(x+3)=x^2+3x$

(b)

	x $+5$
x	x^2+5x

$x(x+5)=x^2+5x$

(c)

	x -2
x	x^2-2x

$x(x-2)=x^2-2x$

(d)

	3 $+2a$
a	$3a+2a^2$

$3a+a^2=a(3+2a)$

(e)

	2 $+3p$
$2p$	$4p+6p^2$

$4p+6p^2=2p(2+3p)$

(f)

	t -3
$3t$	$3t^2-9t$

$3t^2-9t=3t\,(t-3)$

8 (a) $5(a+2)$ (b) $2(2a+1)$ (c) $a(3+b)$
(d) $a(a+2)$ (e) $2b(b+2)$ (f) $3b(1+3b)$
(g) $x(2x-1)$ (h) $x(a-2x)$ (i) $ab(1-b)$
(j) $xy(x+y)$ (k) $2n(m-2n)$ (l) $pq(q^2-2p)$

Exercise 4 p19

1 $a=20$ 2 $a=56$

Assignment 2 Algebraic grids p20

Possible expressions are $a+1$, $a-9$.

Exercise 5 p20

1 $a-5$ or $\frac{3a}{4}$, $3a+10$

2 $\frac{a}{2}$, $a-46$ or $\frac{a}{4}-4$

Exercise 6 p21

1 (a)

	x	$+4$
x	x^2	$+4x$
$+2$	$+2x$	$+8$

$x^2+6x+8=(x+2)(x+4)$

(b)

	x	$+4$
x	x^2	$+4x$
$+1$	$+1x$	$+4$

$x^2+5x+4=(x+1)(x+4)$

(c)

	x	$+5$
x	x^2	$+5x$
$+2$	$+2x$	$+10$

$x^2+7x+10=(x+2)(x+5)$

(d)

	x	-4
x	x^2	$-4x$
$+2$	$+2x$	-8

$x^2-2x-8=(x+2)(x-4)$

2 (a) $x^2+2x+1=(x+1)(x+1)$
(b) $x^2+3x+2=(x+2)(x+1)$
(c) $x^2+6x+9=(x+3)(x+3)$
(d) $x^2+x-2=(x+2)(x-1)$
(e) $x^2-x-6=(x+2)(x-3)$
(f) $x^2-2x+1=(x-1)(x-1)$

3 (a) $x^2+5x+4=(x+1)(x+4)$
(b) $x^2+5x+6=(x+2)(x+3)$
(c) $x^2+4x+4=(x+2)(x+2)$
(d) $x^2+7x+6=(x+6)(x+1)$
(e) $x^2+x-6=(x+3)(x-2)$
(f) $x^2+x-12=(x+4)(x-3)$
(g) $x^2-3x+2=(x-1)(x-2)$
(h) $x^2-3x-10=(x-5)(x+2)$

4 (a) $2c$ (b) b (c) 2 (d) $3h$
(e) $2d+1$ (f) $g+2$ (g) $p+1$ (h) $t+2$

Exercise 7 p22

1 (a) $x+2$ (b) $x+2$ (c) $x-1$ (d) $x-3$
(e) $x+1$ (f) $3x+2$ (g) $2x+1$ (h) $2x+3$

Exercise 8 p23

1 (a) $s=t-3$ (b) $s=t-\frac{1}{4}$ (c) $s=t+6$
(d) $s=t+\frac{1}{2}$ (e) $s=\frac{t}{2}$ (f) $s=\frac{t}{3}$
(g) $s=2t$ (h) $s=3t$ (i) $s=\frac{3}{4}t$

2 (a) $n=\frac{1}{2}(m-1)$ (b) $n=\frac{1}{2}m-1$ (c) $n=\frac{m}{3}+2$
(d) $n=\frac{m+2}{3}$ (e) $n=2(m-2)$ (f) $n=2m-2$
(g) $n=2m-3$ (h) $n=3m+4$ (i) $n=2(m-5)$

3 (a) $s=r-t$ (b) $s=\frac{r}{t}$ (c) $s=\frac{r-3}{t}$
(d) $s=rt$ (e) $s=t(r-2)$ (f) $s=\frac{t+2}{r}$
(g) $s=r+at$ (h) $s=\frac{at}{r}$ (i) $s=\frac{at-2}{r}$

4 (a) $t=r-s$ (b) $t=\frac{r}{s}$ (c) $t=\frac{r-3}{s}$
(d) $t=\frac{s}{r}$ (e) $t=\frac{s}{r-2}$ (f) $t=rs-2$
(g) $t=\frac{s-r}{a}$ (h) $t=\frac{sr}{a}$ (i) $t=\frac{rs+2}{a}$

5 (a) $b=3a-4$ (b) $b=4(a-2)$ (c) $b=\frac{2a-5}{3}$
(d) $b=5(a+2)$ (e) $b=\frac{4a+3}{3}$ (f) $b=\frac{4a-1}{3}$
(g) $b=\frac{3a-1}{2}$ (h) $b=\frac{4a}{3}-2$ (i) $b=\frac{5a+3}{2}$

6 $r=\frac{C}{2\pi}$

7 $r=\sqrt{\frac{A}{\pi}}$

8 $b=\sqrt{(a^2-c^2)}$

9 (a) $t=\sqrt{d}$ (b) $t=d^2$ (c) $t=\sqrt{(d-2)}$
(d) $t=d^2+3$ (e) $t=(d-4)^2$ (f) $t=\sqrt{d}-2$
(g) $t=\frac{\sqrt{d}}{3}$ (h) $t=\frac{d^2+3}{4}$ (i) $t=\frac{\sqrt{d}-4}{5}$

10 (a) $v=u+at$, $u=v-at$, $a=\frac{v-u}{t}$, $t=\frac{v-u}{a}$
(b) $a=b^2+c$, $b=\sqrt{(a-c)}$, $c=a-b^2$
(c) $m=\frac{p-q}{r}$, $p=mr+q$, $q=p-mr$, $r=\frac{p-q}{m}$
(d) $p=\sqrt{(\frac{q-2r}{s})}$, $q=p^2s+2r$, $r=\frac{q-p^2s}{2}$, $s=\frac{q-2r}{p^2}$
(e) $a=b^2+cd$, $c=\frac{a-b^2}{d}$, $d=\frac{a-b^2}{c}$, $b=\sqrt{(a-cd)}$
(f) $a=\frac{v^2-u^2}{2s}$, $s=\frac{v^2-u^2}{2a}$, $u=v-\sqrt{(2as)}$, $v=u+\sqrt{(2as)}$

Exercise 9 p24

1 (a) $1, 2, 4, p, 2p, 4p$
(b) $1, 2, 3, 4, 6, 12, p, 2p, 3p, 4p, 6p, 12p, p^2, 2p^2, 3p^2, 4p^2, 6p^2, 12p^2$
(c) $1, p, q, pq$
(d) $1, 2, 3, 6, p, 2p, 3p, 6p, q, 2q, 3q, 6q, pq, 2pq, 3pq, 6pq$
(e) $1, 2, 4, 8, p, 2p, 4p, 8p, p^2, 2p^2, 4p^2, 8p^2, pq, 2pq, 4pq, 8pq, p^2q, 2p^2q, 4p^2q, 8p^2q$

(f) $1, 2, 3, 6, p, 2p, 3p, 6p, q, 2q, 3q, 6q, pq, 2pq, 3pq, 6pq, p^2q, 2p^2q, 3p^2q, 6p^2q, pq^2, 2pq^2, 3pq^2, 6pq^2, p^2q^2, 2p^2q^2, 3p^2q^2, 6p^2q^2$

2 (a) 1, 2 (b) $1, p$
(c) $1, 2, q, 2q$ (d) $1, 3, q, 3q$
(e) $1, 2, p, 2p, r, 2r, pr, 2pr$ (f) 1, 2

3 (a) $4d + 6 = 2(2d + 3)$ (b) $3b + 5b^2 = b(3 + 5b)$
(c) $6 - 4g = 2(3 - 2g)$ (d) $6b^2 - 3b = 3(2b - 1)$
(e) $2h - 4h^2 = 2h(1 - 2h)$ (f) $ah - bh = h(a - b)$

4 (a) $5(w + 2)$ (b) $a(a + 1)$ (c) $2(2a + 3b)$ (d) $3(3f - 1)$
(e) $2p(2p - 1)$ (f) $b(a + c)$ (g) $2b(a - 2c)$ (h) $3d(c + 2e)$

5 (a) $x^2 + 7x + 12 = (x + 3)(x + 4)$
(b) $x^2 - x - 6 = (x - 3)(x + 2)$
(c) $x^2 + 7x + 10 = (x + 5)(x + 2)$
(d) $x^2 - 5x + 6 = (x - 3)(x - 2)$
(e) $x^2 - 3x - 10 = (x - 5)(x + 2)$
(f) $x^2 + 8x + 7 = (x + 1)(x + 7)$ *or* $x^2 - 8x + 7 = (x - 1)(x - 7)$

6 (a) $(b + 1)(b + 2)$ (b) $(t - 4)(t - 2)$
(c) $(x - 5)(x + 3)$ (d) $(p + 8)(p - 1)$

7 (a) $d = \frac{a+3}{2}$ (b) $d = \frac{m}{3} + 4$ (c) $d = \frac{b-3}{4}$
(d) $d = \frac{p}{5} - 3$ (e) $d = 2t + 3$ (f) $d = 3(k + 2)$
(g) $d = 5h - 3$ (h) $d = \frac{yc}{a}$ (i) $d = \frac{u-c}{a}$
(j) $d = \frac{r+w}{3}$ (k) $d = (st)^2$ (l) $d = \sqrt{(a + b)}$

Chapter 3

Assignment 1 A cross square p26

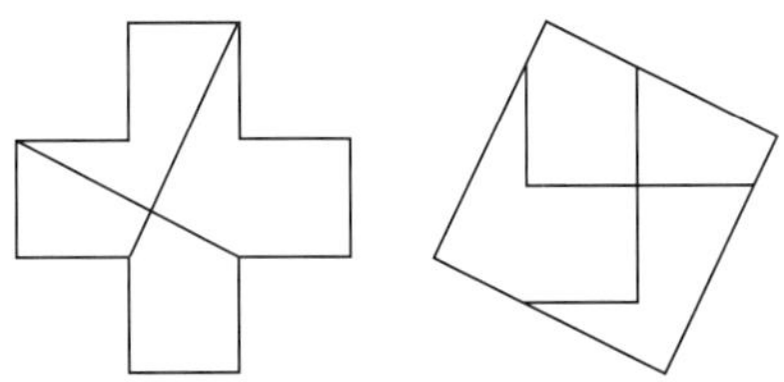

Note: this 4-piece dissection is not unique.

Exercise 1 p26

1 $a = 5.77$; $b = 8.90$ 2 $c = 12.37$
3 $d = 11.07$ 4 $e = 10.73$

Exercise 2 p28

1 $a = 6$ cm; $b = 8.49$ cm; $c = 5.74$ cm; $d = 1.73$ cm; $e = 8.77$ cm; $f = 9.64$ cm
2 AB = 18.03 cm 3 $a = 15.62$ cm; $b = 17.55$ cm
4 55.9 m 5 6.54 m 6 13.42 cm
7 (a) $2b$ cm (b) $\sqrt{5}b$ cm
8 (a) 16 cm (b) 9 cm (c) 15 cm

Exercise 3 p30

1 13.86 cm 2 5.50 m 3 107.24 cm
4 40.93 cm 5 12.04 cm 6 $\sqrt{a^2 + b^2 + c^2}$
7 12.25 cm

8 (b) 11.66 cm (c) 13.11 cm

Assignment 5 Triple search p35

Twenty triples are given below:

3, 4, 5	5, 12, 13	6, 8, 10	7, 24, 25
8, 15, 17	9, 40, 41	10, 24, 26	11, 60, 61
12, 16, 20	12, 35, 37	13, 84, 85	14, 48, 50
15, 112, 113	16, 30, 34	20, 21, 29	20, 48, 52
24, 32, 40	27, 36, 45	28, 45, 53	39, 52, 65

Assignment 7 Making Plato's triples p35

When $m = 1$, the triple is (0,2,2).
When $m = 2$, the triple is (3,4,5).
When $m = 3$, the triple is (8,6,10).
When $m = 4$, the triple is (15,8,17).
When $m = 5$, the triple is (24,10,26).
Not all triples are possible; except when $m = 2$, triples involving differences of 1 are impossible.

Assignment 8 Making Euclid's triples p35

See triples list in Assignment 7.
All triples contain at least one number which is a multiple of 3, 4 or 5. It is possible to prove this using Euclid's triple.

Chapter 4

Exercise 1 p36

1 (a) $1152 \div 7 = 164.6$ cm (to 1 d.p.)
(b) Median = 163 cm
(c) Mode = 169 cm
(d) Range = 17 cm

2 (a)

Number of hours	Frequency	Total time spent
$\frac{1}{2}$ hour	2	1
1 hour	8	8
$1\frac{1}{2}$ hours	17	25.5
2 hours	19	38
$2\frac{1}{2}$ hours	4	10
Total	50	82.5

(b) Mean = 1.65 hours or 1 hour 39 minutes; Median = 1.5 hours; Mode = 2 hours

3 (a) Mean = 27.9 marks
(b) Range = 54 − 8 = 46 (marks)
(c)

Group	Frequency
0–19	10
20–39	15
40–60	6

(d)

Group	Frequency
0–11	3
12–23	8
24–35	12
36–47	6
48–60	2

(e)

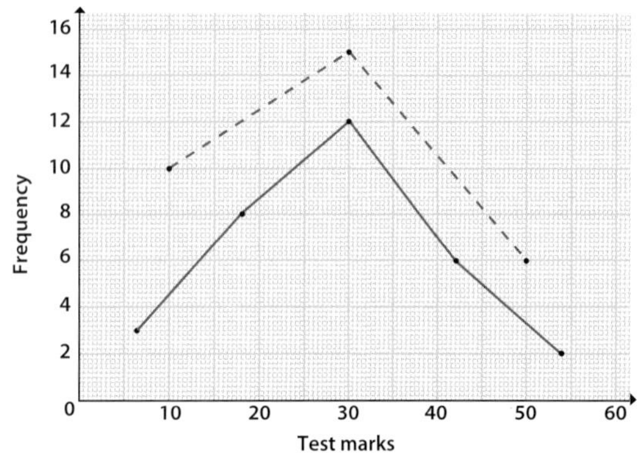

Using five groups gives more information. It shows that fewer pupils scored the lowest marks and shows more clearly the distribution at the higher scores.

Exercise 2

p38

1 (a)

Time (t sec)	Frequency	Mid-interval value	Mid-interval value × frequency
$0 \leq t < 2$	15	1	15
$2 \leq t < 4$	31	3	93
$4 \leq t < 6$	9	5	45
$6 \leq t < 8$	4	7	28
$8 \leq t < 10$	1	9	9
	Total 60		Total 190

(b) Estimated mean = 3.17 minutes

2

Money raised (£ r)	Frequency	Mid-interval value £	Mid-interval value × frequency £
$0 \leq r < 10$	18	5	90
$2 \leq r < 20$	30	15	450
$4 \leq r < 30$	23	25	575
$6 \leq r < 40$	17	35	595
$8 \leq r < 50$	12	45	540
	Total 100		Total: £2250

Estimated mean = £22.50

3 (a)

Test scores m	Frequency	Mid-interval value	Mid-interval value × frequency
$0 \leq m < 12$	3	6	18
$12 \leq m < 24$	8	18	144
$24 \leq m < 36$	12	30	360
$36 \leq m < 48$	6	42	252
$48 \leq m < 60$	2	54	108
	Total 31		Total 882

(b) Estimated mean = 28.5

(c) The estimated mean is only 0.6 greater than the actual mean. Only a small error for considerably less calculation.

Exercise 3

p40

1 (a) Total time = 32 hours 44 minutes;
mean = 3 hours 16 minutes

(b) Range = 2 hours 30 minutes

(c) 20%

(d) The mean is not a good measure of average.
The distribution of the data is affected by the one runner who took much longer.

2 (a) Mean = 65 children / 40 families
≅ 1.6 children per family

Number of children	Frequency	Total for group
0	6	6
1	12	12
2	17	34
3	2	6
4	2	8
5	1	5

(b) Range = 5 children

(c) The bar chart shows clearly that most families had none, one or two children. Very few families had more than two children.

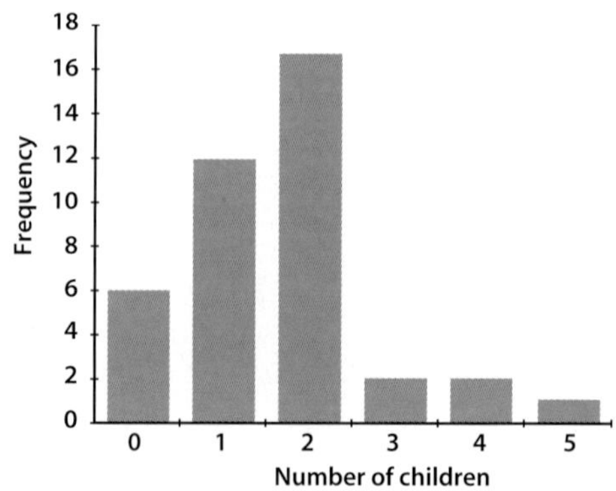

(d) 55% of families have more than the average number of children.

Exercise 4 p41

1

Money raised (£ *r*)	Frequency	Money raised (£ *r*)	Cumulative frequency
$0 \leq r < 10$	18	$r < 10$	18
$10 \leq r < 20$	30	$r < 20$	48
$20 \leq r < 30$	23	$r < 30$	71
$30 \leq r < 40$	17	$r < 40$	88
$40 \leq r < 50$	12	$r < 50$	100

Median = £22

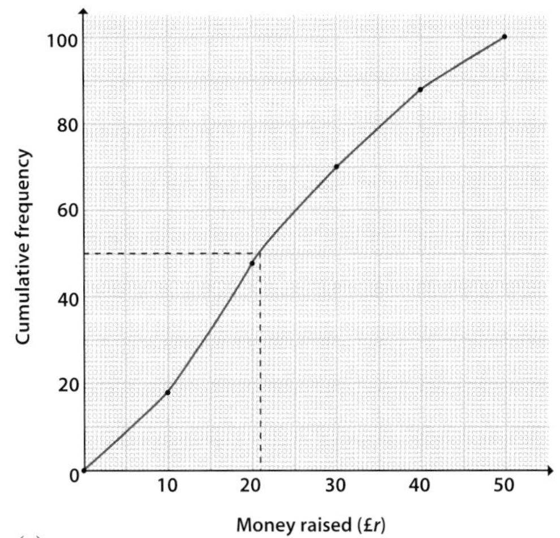

2 (a)

Weight (*w* kg)	Frequency	Weight (*w* kg)	Cumulative frequency
$40 \leq w < 45$	18	$w < 45$	3
$45 \leq w < 50$	30	$w < 50$	5
$50 \leq w < 55$	23	$w < 55$	9
$55 \leq w < 60$	17	$w < 60$	26
$60 \leq w < 65$	12	$w < 65$	70
$65 \leq w < 70$	12	$w < 70$	90
$70 \leq w < 75$	12	$w < 75$	95

(b)

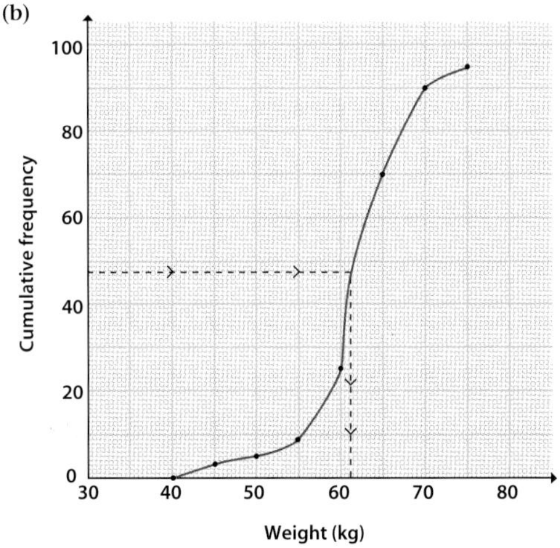

Median = 61.5 kg, but answers will depend on graph. From the table alone, median = 62.5 kg.

3 (a)

Time (*t* hours)	Frequency	Time spent	Cumulative frequency
$5 \leq t < 10$	5	< 10	5
$10 \leq t < 15$	12	< 15	17
$15 \leq t < 20$	21	< 20	38
$20 \leq t < 25$	25	< 25	63
$25 \leq t < 30$	18	< 30	81
$30 \leq t < 35$	9	< 35	90

(b)

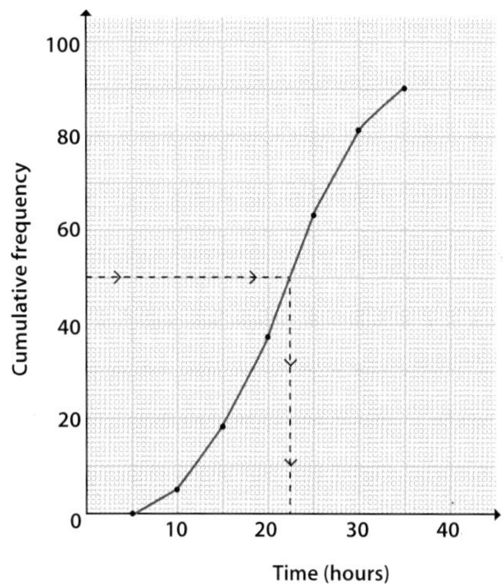

Median = 22 hours, but answers will depend on graph. From the table alone, median = 21.4 hours.

Exercise 5 p43

1 (a) Median = 6.5

(b) Lower quartile = 5; upper quartile = 9

(c) Interquartile range = 4

2

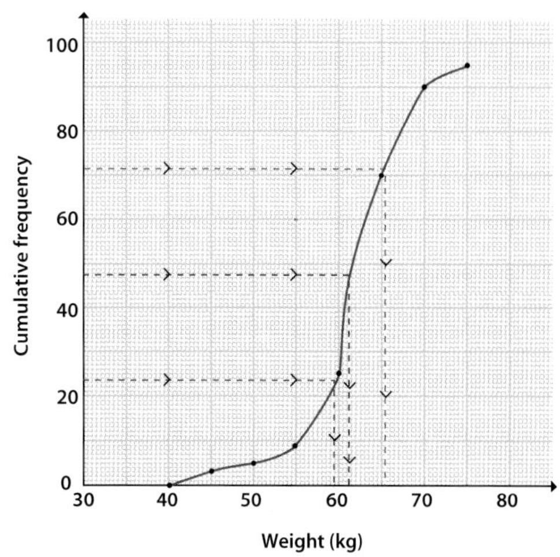

(a) Lower quartile = 59.5 kg

(b) Upper quartile = 65.5 kg

(c) Interquartile range = 6 kg

3

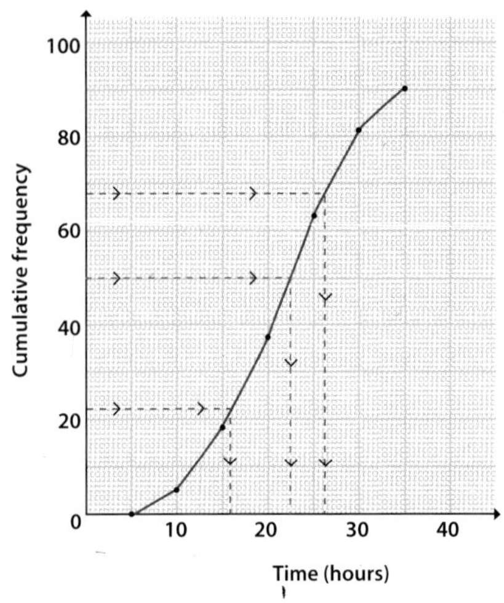

(a) Lower quartile = 16.5 hours

(b) Upper quartile = 26.5 hours

(c) Interquartile range = 10 hours

5

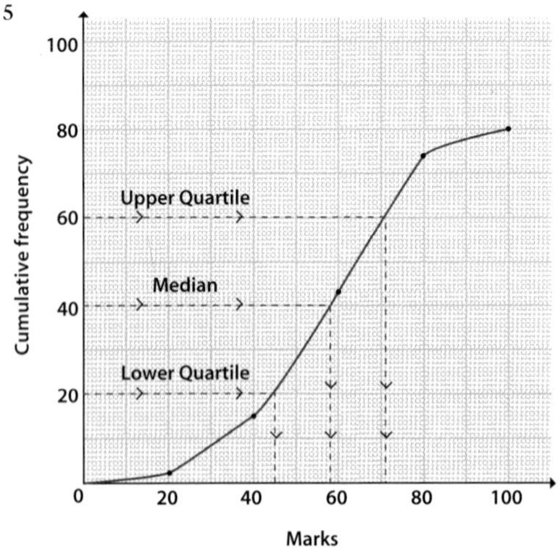

(a) (i) Median = 58 marks (ii) lower quartile = 45 marks; upper quartile = 71 marks (iii) interquartile range = 26 marks

(b) 66% (c) 78 marks (d) 73 marks

Assignment 2 Understanding the box plot p44

Interquartile range is included in the box.

Median is marked by the line inside the box.

The whiskers show the greatest and smallest values, i.e. the range.

The ends of the box show the lower and upper quartiles.

A box plot helps to show how the IQ range fits into the whole range and also where the median fits within the IQ range.

Exercise 6 p44

1 (a)

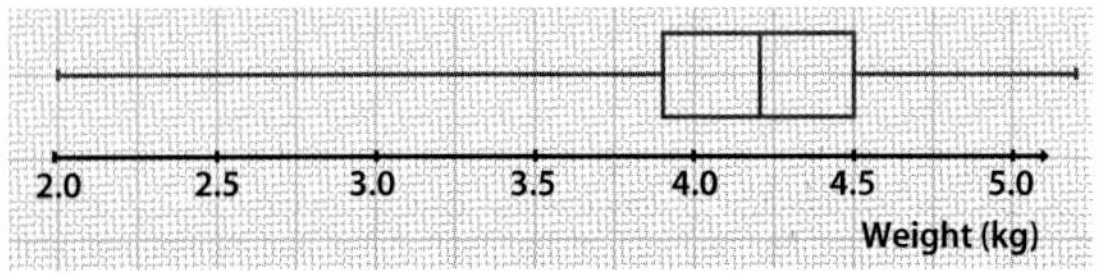

(b) The box plot shows the very wide range. However as the IQ range is very small, 50% of the total number of fish weighed similar amounts.

2 (a)

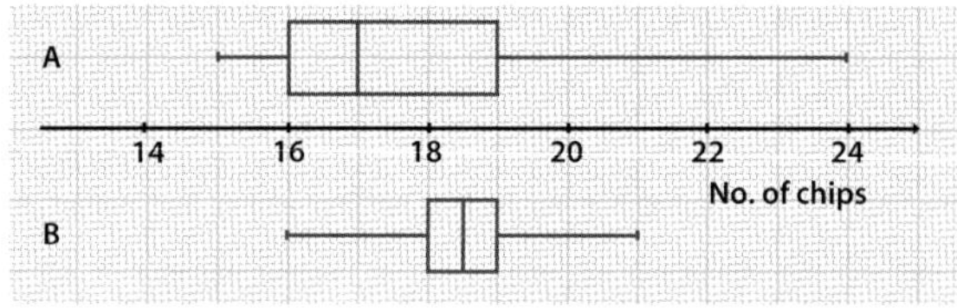

(b) Assistant A serves very varied sizes of portions whereas assistant B is more consistent. This can be seen by considering the ranges and IQ ranges. However since B's median is greater than A's, more pupils get more chips more often. The final choice will depend on the risk you are prepared to take!

3 (a)

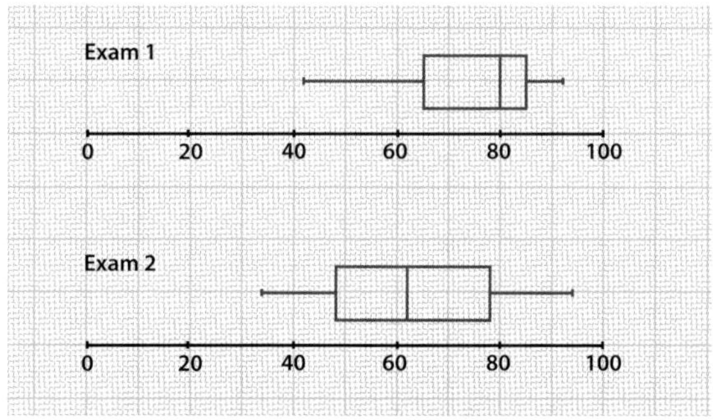

(b) The pupils found the first examination to be easier than the second (more pupils obtaining higher marks). The interquartile range on the first was smaller showing less spread of the students which shows up also in the smaller range. The second examination would be more useful to identify problems.

Assignment 3 Comparing pulse rates p45

Measuring the time taken for 60 beats allows the collection of continuous data. The degree of accuracy, the reasons for the choice of statistical display and appropriate average should be discussed.

Chapter 5

Assignment 1 Lengths of tangent sections p46

Answers are obtained by reading values from a graph and are likely, therefore, to vary slightly from those listed here.

Angle	Length of tangent section
0°	0.00
10°	0.18
20°	0.36
30°	0.58
40°	0.84
50°	1.20
60°	1.73
70°	2.75

Things to notice:

- As angle increases, so does the length of the tangent section.
- Length of tangent section for 90° is infinite (∞).

Exercise 1 p48

$b = 0.36$; $c = 0.84$; $d = 0.58$; $e = 1.73$; $f = 50°$; $g = 10°$; $h = 70$; $i = 1.00$

Exercise 2 p49

1 (a) 0.625 (b) 1.48 (c) 57.3 (d) 0.225
(e) 4.79 (f) 0.0752 (g) 573 (h) 0.760
(i) 0.00157 (j) 1.17 (k) 1.00 (l) 2.00

2 (a) 42.0° (b) 76.0° (c) 39.0° (d) 81.0°
(e) 32.2° (f) 55.4° (g) 68.2° (h) 40.9°
(i) 36.9° (j) 31.0° (k) 26.6° (l) 60.0°

3 $\tan 90° = \infty$

Exercise 3 p50

$a = 6.01$; $b = 2.65$; $c = 0.626$; $d = 5.01$; $e = 35.3$; $f = 21.6$; $g = 55.6$; $h = 0.779$; $i = 2.12$; $j = 0.300$

Exercise 4 p51

$a = 35.0°$; $b = 54.0°$; $c = 28.8°$; $d = 23.7°$; $e = 48.8°$; $f = 33.7°$; $g = 67.5°$; $h = 41.8°$

Assignment 2 Coordinate points on a circle p52

Angle	x	y
0°	1.00	0.00
10°	0.98	0.17
20°	0.94	0.34
30°	0.87	0.50
40°	0.77	0.64
50°	0.64	0.77
60°	0.50	0.87
70°	0.34	0.94
80°	0.17	0.98
90°	0.00	1.00

Exercise 5 p53

$a = 0.87$; $b = 0.50$; $c = 0.64$; $d = 0.77$; $e = 60°$; $f = 80°$; $g = 0.94$; $h = 0.34$; $i = 0.77$; $j = 0.64$; $k = 10°$

Exercise 6 p54

$a = 4.19$; $b = 6.36$; $c = 9.34$; $d = 3.58$; $e = 4.69$; $f = 8.13$; $g = 4.49$; $h = 24.6$; $i = 2.27$; $j = 13.7$

Exercise 7 p55

$a = 53.1°$; $b = 41.4°$; $c = 51.3°$; $d = 58.2°$; $e = 33.7°$; $f = 58.4°$; $g = 44.7°$; $h = 39.6°$

Exercise 8 p56

a = hyp; b = adj; c = opp d = opp; e = adj; f = hyp
g = adj; h = hyp; i = opp j = opp; k = hyp; l = adj
XY = adj; XZ = opp; YZ = hyp

Exercise 9 p58

$b = 13.5$; $c = 14.5$; $d = 5.06$; $e = 9.37$; $f = 1.47$; $g = 66.2°$; $h = 70.4°$; $i = 43.2°$

Exercise 10 p59

1 45.5 m 2 Height = 7.99 m; distance = 2.91 m
3 37.3 km 4 50.7°
5 (a) 4.62 cm (b) 9.24 cm 6 150 m
7 (a) AD = 8.66 cm (b) 43.3 cm^2
8 (a) QU = 35.4 m (b) RU = 54.5 m
(c) PT = 19.8 m (d) 4230 m^2

Chapter 6

Exercise 1 p61

1 (c) Book costs £7; magazine costs £3.
2 (b) $d + 2s = 1.70$ (c) $d = 50$; $s = 60$
3 (a) $a = 9$; $b = 2$ (b) $a = 4$; $b = 1$ (c) $a = 5$; $b = 3$
(d) $a = 8$; $b = -2$ (e) $a = 1\frac{1}{2}$; $b = 2$
4 (a) $3a + 2c = 37.7$; $2a + 4c = 40.6$
(b) £8.70 (c) £5.80

Exercise 2 p63

1 (a)

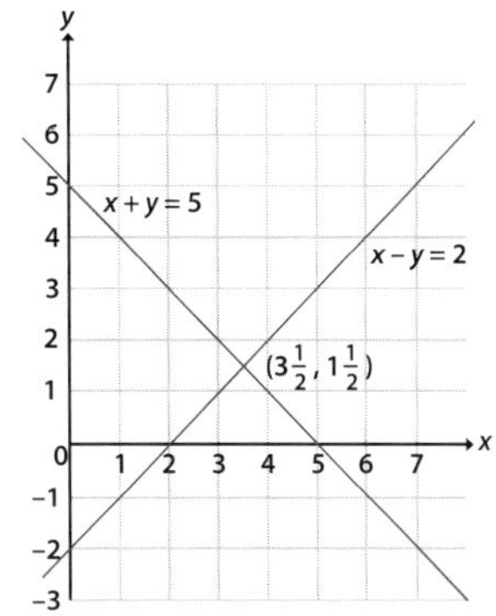

(b) $(3\frac{1}{2}, 1\frac{1}{2})$ (c) $x = 3\frac{1}{2}$; $y = 1\frac{1}{2}$

2 (c)

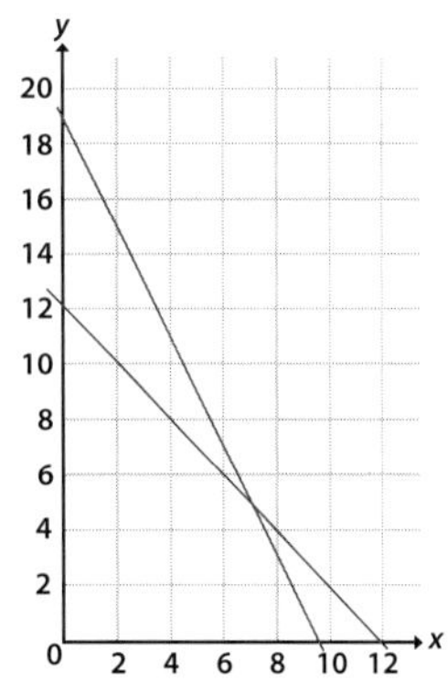

(d) $x = 7$; $y = 5$

3 (a)

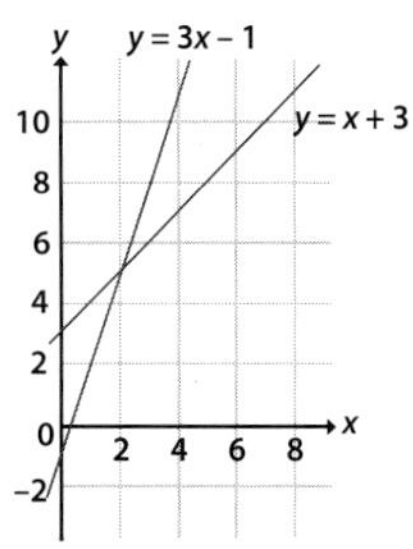

$x = 2, y = 5$

(b)

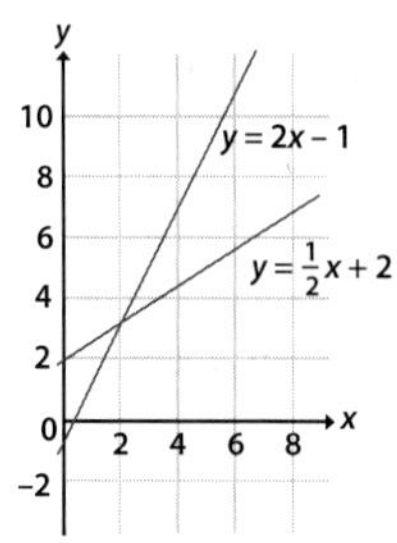

$x = 2, y = 3$

(c)

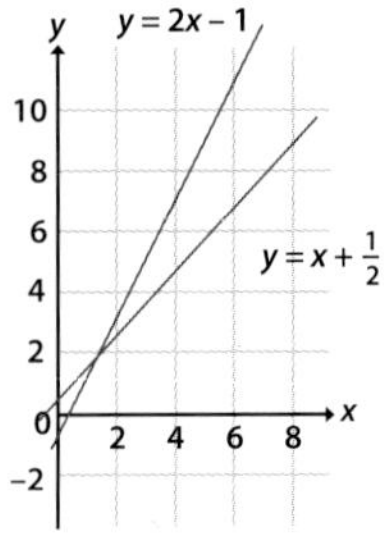

$x = 1\frac{1}{2}, y = 2$

(d)

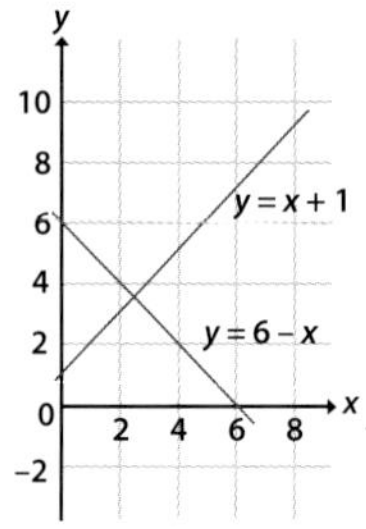

$x = 2\frac{1}{2}, y = 3\frac{1}{2}$

4 (a)

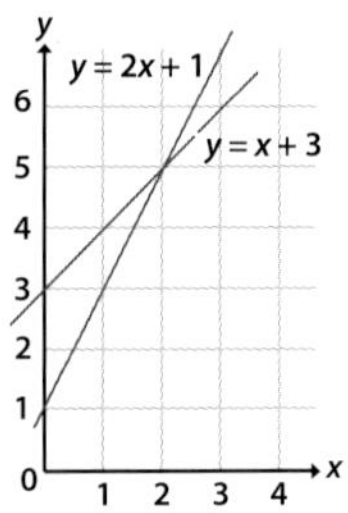

$x = 2, y = 5$

(b)

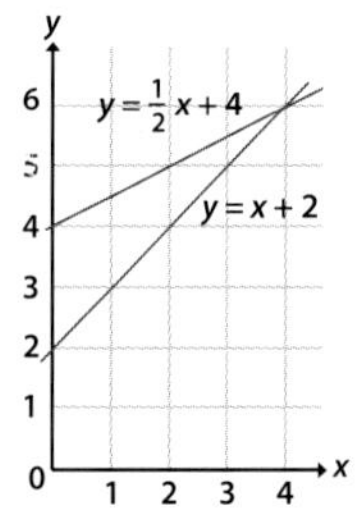

$x = 4, y = 6$

(c)

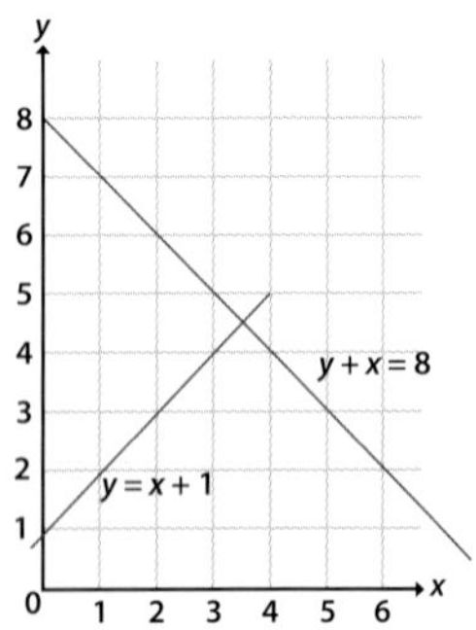

$x = 3\frac{1}{2}, y = 4\frac{1}{2}$

(d)

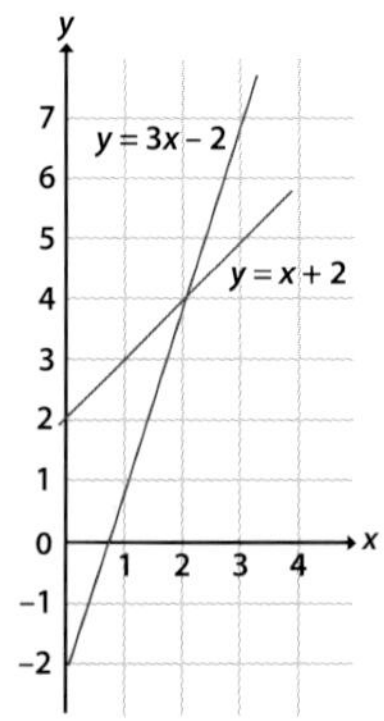

$x = 2, y = 4$

Exercise 3 p65

1 (a) $a = 2; b = 1$ (b) $x = 4; y = 2$ (c) $c = 3; d = 1$
(d) $e = 7; f = 2$ (e) $m = 10; n = 3$ (f) $p = 4; q = 1$
(g) $s = 3; r = 1$ (h) $t = 2; u = -3$ (i) $v = -4; w = 2$
(j) $a = \frac{1}{2}; b = -3$

Exercise 4 p67

1 (a) $x = 2; y = 6$ (b) $m = 3; n = 2$ (c) $e = 4; f = 5$
(d) $a = 6; b = 2$ (e) $a = 3; b = 1$ (f) $s = 3; r = 6$
(g) $u = 5; v = 1$ (h) $m = 5; n = 2$
2 (a) $x = 3; y = 1$ (b) $n = 3; m = 2$ (c) $a = 8; b = 3$
(d) $e = 0.8; f = 0.6$ (e) $q = 3; r = 2$ (f) $d = 7; c = 4$
(g) $a = 2; b = -1$ (h) $a = 6; b = -2$ (i) $s = 1\frac{1}{2}; r = \frac{1}{2}$
(j) $u = 1; v = -1$ (k) $m = \frac{1}{2}; n = 2$ (l) $x = \frac{1}{4}; y = 1$
3 (a) $x = 4; y = 2$ (b) $a = 5; b = 4$ (c) $r = 7; t = 3$
(d) $x = 3; y = \frac{1}{4}$ (e) $z = 8; x = 3$ (f) $a = \frac{1}{3}; b = 0$
(g) $w = 3; v = 2$ (h) $a = 2; b = 4$ (i) $n = -1; m =$
(j) $r = \frac{1}{2}; p = -\frac{1}{2}$ (k) $a = 1; b = 5$ (l) $x = 2; y = 1$
(m) $g = 15; f = 3$ (n) $c = 1; d = 2$

Exercise 5 p69

1 (a) $a = 3; b = 2$ (b) $c = 2, d = \frac{1}{2}$ (c) $m = 2, n = -1$
(d) $p = 2, q = 1$ (e) $h = 1, j = -2$ (f) $x = 1, y = 1$
(g) $j = \frac{1}{3}, k = -\frac{1}{2}$ (h) $a = 1, b = \frac{1}{2}$ (i) $r = \frac{1}{2}, s = 1$
(j) $u = -2, v = -3$ (k) $x = \frac{1}{3}, y = -\frac{1}{2}$ (l) $s = 4, p = -1$
(m) $m = -2, n = \frac{1}{2}$ (n) $a = \frac{1}{2}, b = \frac{1}{4}$ (o) $f = 3, g = -0.6$
(p) $b = 0.4, c = 1.2$ (q) $p = -0.2, q = 0.1$
(r) $v = -1.6, w = -2.2$

Exercise 6 p70

1 (a) $a = 18; b = 7$ (b) $a = 5; b = 6$ (c) $a = -3; b = 4$
2 I: 10 pence; II: 30 pence
3 Child: £1.50; adult: £2.50

Exercise 7 p70

1 (a) $b = 4; a = 10$ (b) $x = 3; y = 10$ (c) $m = 1; n = 1$
2 (a) $a = 3; b = 1$ (b) $x = 7; y = 3$ (c) $m = 2; n = -1$
(d) $r = 0; p = 2$ (e) $b = -1; a = 6$ (f) $x = 7; y = 3$
3 (a) $w = £250; s = £325$ (b) $y = 60; x = 40$
4 (a) (i) $y = 2x - 1$, $y = x + 2$ (ii) $y = x + 1$, $y = \frac{1}{2}x + 3$
(b) (i) $x = 3, y = 5$ (ii) $x = 4, y = 5$

Assignment 1 Polygon patterns p71

When n = 3, $9a + 3b = 12$
$a = 2, b = -2$
Sequence is $2n^2 - 2n + 1$

Chapter 7

Exercise 1 p72

1 (a) $\frac{7}{15}$ (b) $\frac{5}{15} = \frac{1}{3}$ (c) $\frac{5}{15} = \frac{1}{3}$
2 (a) $\frac{5}{7}$ (b) $\frac{4}{6} = \frac{2}{3}$ (c) $\frac{8}{12} = \frac{2}{3}$
3 (a) $\frac{5}{7}$ (b) $\frac{1}{5}$ (c) $\frac{7}{9}$
4 (a) $\frac{1}{3}$ (b) $\frac{2}{25}$ (c) $\frac{5}{36}$
(d) $\frac{1}{28}$ (e) $\frac{2}{27}$ (f) $\frac{9}{20}$
5 $\frac{5}{12}$ 6 $\frac{31}{36}$ 7 $\frac{6}{21} = \frac{2}{7}$

Assignment 1 Three throws of a dice p74

Eight routes are possible.

Exercise 2 p74

1 (a) 1 way (b) 2 ways (c) 1 way
2 3 heads – 1 way 2 heads – 3 ways
1 head – 3 ways 0 heads – 1 way
3 4 heads – 1 way 3 heads – 4 ways
2 heads – 6 ways 1 head – 4 ways 0 heads – 1 way

Assignment 2 More throws p75

n throws – 2^n

Assignment 3
Calculating probabilities from a tree diagram p77

Total probability of all outcomes = 1

For just one six, outcomes are:

six, not a six, not a six

not a six, six, not a six

not a six, six, not a six, six

Probability of each route = $\frac{25}{216}$

P(one six in three throws) = $\frac{75}{216}$

One outcome has no sixes

P(no sixes) = $\frac{125}{216}$

Total probability of all eight outcomes = 1

Exercise 3 p78

1 (a) $\frac{4}{10} = \frac{2}{5}$ (b) $1 - \frac{2}{5} = \frac{3}{5}$

(c) (i) Probability the darts player hits each time =

P(3 bulls) = $\frac{8}{125}$

(ii) P(2 bulls and one miss) = $\frac{12}{125}$

Probability of 2 hits out of 3 = $\frac{36}{125}$

2 (a) $\frac{3}{4}$ on time

(b) $\frac{1}{4}$ late

(c) P(on time 3 times) = $\frac{27}{64}$

(d) P(on time, on time, not on time) = $\frac{9}{64}$

(e) P(2 out of 3 times) = $\frac{27}{64}$

3 (b) P(frost each night) = $\frac{1}{81}$

(c) P(2 out of four) = $\frac{24}{81}$

4 (a) P(late) = $\frac{2}{3}$

(b)

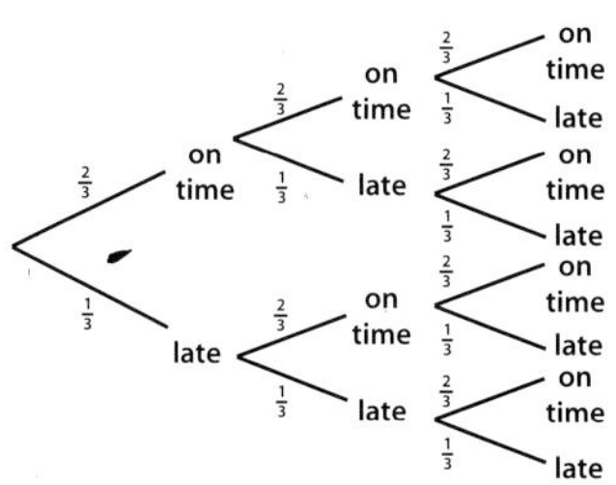

(c) P(late, two out of three times) = $\frac{2}{9}$

(d) P(on time, three times) = $\frac{8}{27}$

Exercise 4 p80

1 (a) $\frac{7}{25} \times \frac{6}{24} = \frac{42}{600} = \frac{7}{100}$ (b) $\frac{8}{25} \times \frac{7}{24} = \frac{56}{600} = \frac{7}{75}$

(c) $\frac{3}{25} \times \frac{2}{24} = \frac{6}{600} = \frac{1}{100}$

2 (a) $\frac{7}{120}$ (b) $\frac{7}{75}$ (c) $\frac{7}{300}$

3 (a) $\frac{1}{460}$ (b) $\frac{1}{460}$ (c) order does not matter

4 (a) $\frac{42}{13800} = \frac{7}{2300}$ (b) $\frac{168}{13800} = \frac{7}{575}$

Outcomes **Probability**

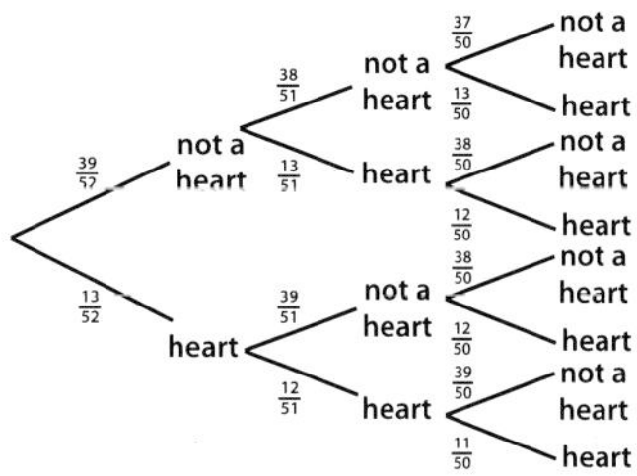

5 (a) $\frac{840}{303600} = \frac{7}{2530}$

(b) $\frac{1176}{303600} = \frac{49}{12650}$

(c) $\frac{30}{303600} = \frac{1}{10120}$

6 (b) (i) P(3 hearts) = $\frac{11}{850}$

(ii) P(at least 2 hearts) = $\frac{128}{850} = \frac{64}{425}$

(iii) P(exactly one heart) = $\frac{741}{1700}$

7 (a) $\frac{5}{10} = \frac{1}{2}$

(b) $\frac{120}{5040} = \frac{1}{42}$

(c) $4 \times \frac{300}{5040} + \frac{120}{5040} = \frac{11}{42} = 0.262$

Exercise 5 p82

1 (a) Event A is independent of Event B.

(b) The events are not mutually exclusive, because both can happen at the same time.

(c) (i) P(A) = $\frac{4}{52} = \frac{1}{13}$ (ii) P(B) = $\frac{1}{6}$

(iii) P(A or B) = P(A but not B) + P(B but not A) + P(A and B)

$= \frac{18}{78} = \frac{3}{13}$

(iv) P(A and B) = P(A) × P(B) = $\frac{1}{78}$

2 (a) Only one card is drawn, so only one of the two events can happen. The probability of each is not dependent on the other.

(b) The events are mutually exclusive (a card cannot be a king and a queen at the same time).

(c) (i) P(X) = $\frac{1}{13}$

(ii) P(Y) = $\frac{1}{13}$

(iii) P(X or Y) = P(X) + P(Y) = $\frac{2}{13}$

(iv) P(X and Y) = 0

3 (a) P(late) = $\frac{1}{5}$

(b) P(early and crossing safely) = $\frac{36}{50}$

(c) P(late and crossing safely) = $\frac{1}{20}$

(d) P(early and run over) = $\frac{4}{50}$

(e) P(crossing safely) = $\frac{77}{100}$

4 (a) P(2 red) = $\frac{1}{16}$ (b) P(2 green) = $\frac{25}{144}$

(c) P(1 black and 1 green) = $\frac{20}{144}$

(d) P(2 same) = $\frac{50}{144}$

5 (a)

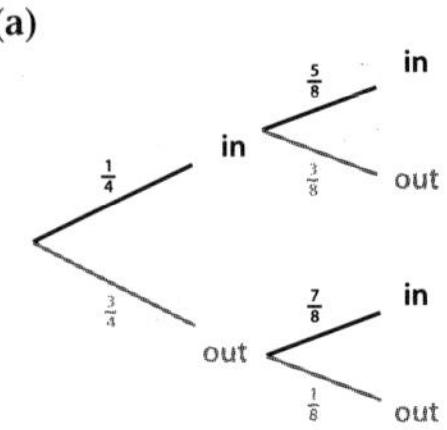

(b) P(out both nights) = $\frac{3}{4} \times \frac{1}{8} = \frac{3}{52}$

(c) P(in on only one night) = $\left(\frac{1}{4} \times \frac{3}{8}\right) + \left(\frac{3}{4} \times \frac{7}{8}\right) = \frac{3}{32} + \frac{21}{32}$
$= \frac{24}{32} = \frac{3}{4}$

Assignment 4 Making a profit p83

Win with (8,9,10) (7,9,10) (6,9,10); P(winning) $\frac{4}{720} = \frac{1}{180}$;
Bad game, as there is a very small probability of winning only 50p.

Chapter 8

Assignment 1
Plotting the relationship between x and y p84

x	0	1	2	3	4	5	6
y	0	1	4	9	16	25	36

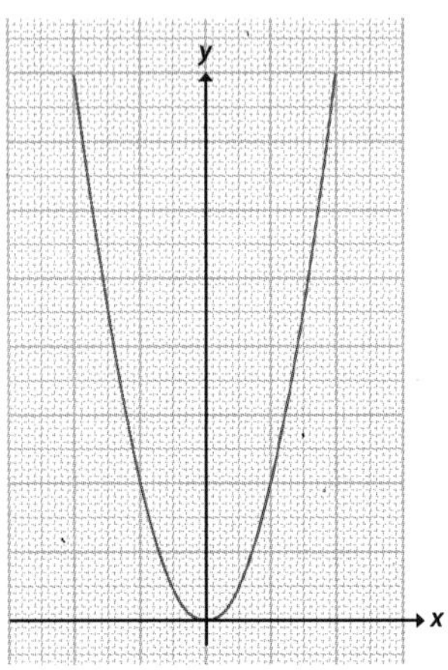

Equation of mirror line: y axis, $x = 0$
$3.5^2 = 12.25$
$\sqrt{64} = \pm 8$

Exercise 1 p85

1 (a) ±9.5 (b) 46.2 (c) 5.76
(d) ±5.5 (e) ±7 (f) 1

Assignment 2 Conic sections p85

Conic sections: circle, ellipse, parabola, hyperbola

Assignment 3 Constructing a table of values p86

$y = x^2 + 2$ cuts the y axis at $y = 2$
$y = x^2 + 4$ cuts the y axis at $y = 4$
$y = x^2 - 4$ cuts the y axis at $y = -4$

Assignment 4 The family of parabolas p86

Coefficients greater than 1 make a narrower curve; fractional coefficients make a wider curve; negative coefficients produce an inverted curve.

Exercise 2 p86

1 (a) $x = 0, y = 0; x = -4, y = -32; x = 3, y = -18; x = 5, y = -50; x = -2, y = -8$

(b)

x	−4	−3	−2	−1	0	1	2	3	4
y	−32	−18	−8	−2	0	−2	−8	−18	−32

(d) $y = -40, x \cong \pm 4.5; y = -20, x \cong \pm 3.2$
(e) $x = -3.5, y = -24.5; x = -1.5, y = -4.5$

2

x	−4	−3	−2	−1	0	1	2	3	4
y	−8	$-4\frac{1}{2}$	−2	$-\frac{1}{2}$	0	$\frac{1}{2}$	2	$4\frac{1}{2}$	8

Exercise 3 p88

1

x	−3	−2	−1	0	1	2	3
x^2	9	4	1	0	1	4	9
$2x^2$	18	8	2	0	2	8	18
+4	+4	4	4	4	4	4	4
y	22	12	6	4	6	12	22

2

x → [x^2] → [×3] → [−2] → [y]

x	−3	−2	−1	0	1	2	3	4
x^2	9	4	1	0	1	4	9	16
$3x^2$	27	12	3	0	3	12	27	48
−2	−2	−2	−2	−2	−2	−2	−2	−2
y	25	10	1	−2	1	10	25	46

3

x	−3	−2	−1	0	1	2	3	4
x^2	9	4	1	0	1	4	9	16
$4x^2$	36	16	4	0	4	16	36	64
−2	−2	−2	−2	−2	−2	−2	−2	−2
y	34	14	2	−2	2	14	34	62

4 The graph of $y = 3x^2 - 2$ cuts the y axis at (0, –2).
The graph of $y = 4x^2 - 2$ also cuts the y axis at (0, –2).
The graph of $y = 4x^2 - 2$ is narrower than the graph of $y = 3x^2 - 2$.

Assignment 5 Drawing graphs of $y = (x + b)^2$ p88

x	–3	–2	–1	0	1	2	3	4	5
$x + 2$	–1	0	1	2	3	4	5	6	7
$(x + 2)^2$	1	0	1	4	9	16	25	36	49

When $y = 0$, $x = -2$
When $x = 0$, $y = 4$

Exercise 4 p88

1 (a)

x	–6	–5	–4	–3	–2	–1	0	1	2	3	4	5	6
y	4	1	0	1	4	9	16	25	36	49	64	81	100

(c) When $x = 0$, $y = 16$
(d) When $y = 0$, $x = -4$

2 (a)

x	–3	–2	–1	0	1	2	3	4	5	6
y	36	25	16	9	4	1	0	1	4	9

(c) Curve touches axis at $x = 3$
3 (a) $y = 25$ (b) $x = 5$ (c) $x = 5$

Exercise 5 p90

2 (a) $y = x^2 + 3$ (b) $y = x^2 - 5$ (c) $y = -x^2 + 2$
(d) $y = \frac{1}{2}x^2 + 2$ (e) $y = (x + 1)^2$ (f) $y = (x - 7)^2$

Assignment 7 Investigating curves p92

Higher powers of x produce different shaped curves.
$x^2 + 4x + 4 = (x + 2)^2$